TAGHEUER.COM
PORSCHE
CARRERA
TAG HEUER

HOTEL BELVEDERE

INTRO

CURVES Schweiz. Was für ein Wiedersehen mit diesem einzigartigen Land in der Mitte Europas, das immer auch ein starkes Synonym für „Berge“ ist. Und ganz besonders für „Gran Turismo“ – das Überqueren der Berge zwischen Nord und Süd, auf der Suche nach einem Weg, der zum Ziel wird. Dabei folgt diese CURVES-Ausgabe überhaupt nicht jener altbekannten Sehnsuchtsroute der Automobilisten, sondern sie nimmt es mit nahezu der gesamten Schweiz auf. Fährt vom Stilfser Joch an der Grenze bei Österreich und Italien bis hinunter in den äußersten Südwesten am Grand-Saint-Bernard. Unterteilt in fünf starke Etappen, von denen jede ihre ganz eigene Herausforderung, individuellen Reiz und ganz eigenen Charakter hat. Als klassisches Thema aller Reisenden aus Leidenschaft werden die großen Routen der Schweiz in dieser Ausgabe neu erzählt. CURVES kommt damit ein klein wenig nach Hause, schließlich ist die Schweiz nicht nur Inspiration für die Entstehung dieses Magazins und nun bereits zum dritten Mal Inhalt und Ziel von CURVES, sondern auch eine absolute Herzens-Destination unserer Leser. Fahren Sie mit uns zwischen Graubünden und Vaud, Bern und Tessin, entdecken Sie die ewig jungen Helden Gotthard, Grimselpass und Stelvio, kommen Sie mit uns in die Schweiz. Grüezi und Bun Viadi, Happy Soulful Driving.

—

CURVES Switzerland. What magical a reunion with this unique country in the heart of Europe, which is always been synonymous with “the mountains” and, more especially, with “Gran Turismo” – crossing the mountains between north and south in an exercise in which the route itself becomes the reward. This edition of CURVES doesn’t follow the familiar route so beloved by most motorists, but instead takes in almost the whole of Switzerland. It takes us from the Stilfser Joch on the border with Austria and Italy down to the extreme southwest on the Great-Saint Bernard Pass. Our tour is divided into five lively stages, each of which has its own challenges, individual charms and character. A classic theme for all passionate travelers, we relive the great routes of Switzerland in this issue. For CURVES this is a little bit of a homecoming. After all, Switzerland was not only the inspiration for the creation of this magazine, now providing content for CURVES for the third time, but also a favorite destination for our readers. Join us on this trip between Graubünden and Vaud, Bern and Ticino. Discover the undying heroes of the Gotthard, Grimsel and Stelvio Passes. Come with us to Switzerland. Grüezi and Bun Viadi! Happy Soulful Driving.

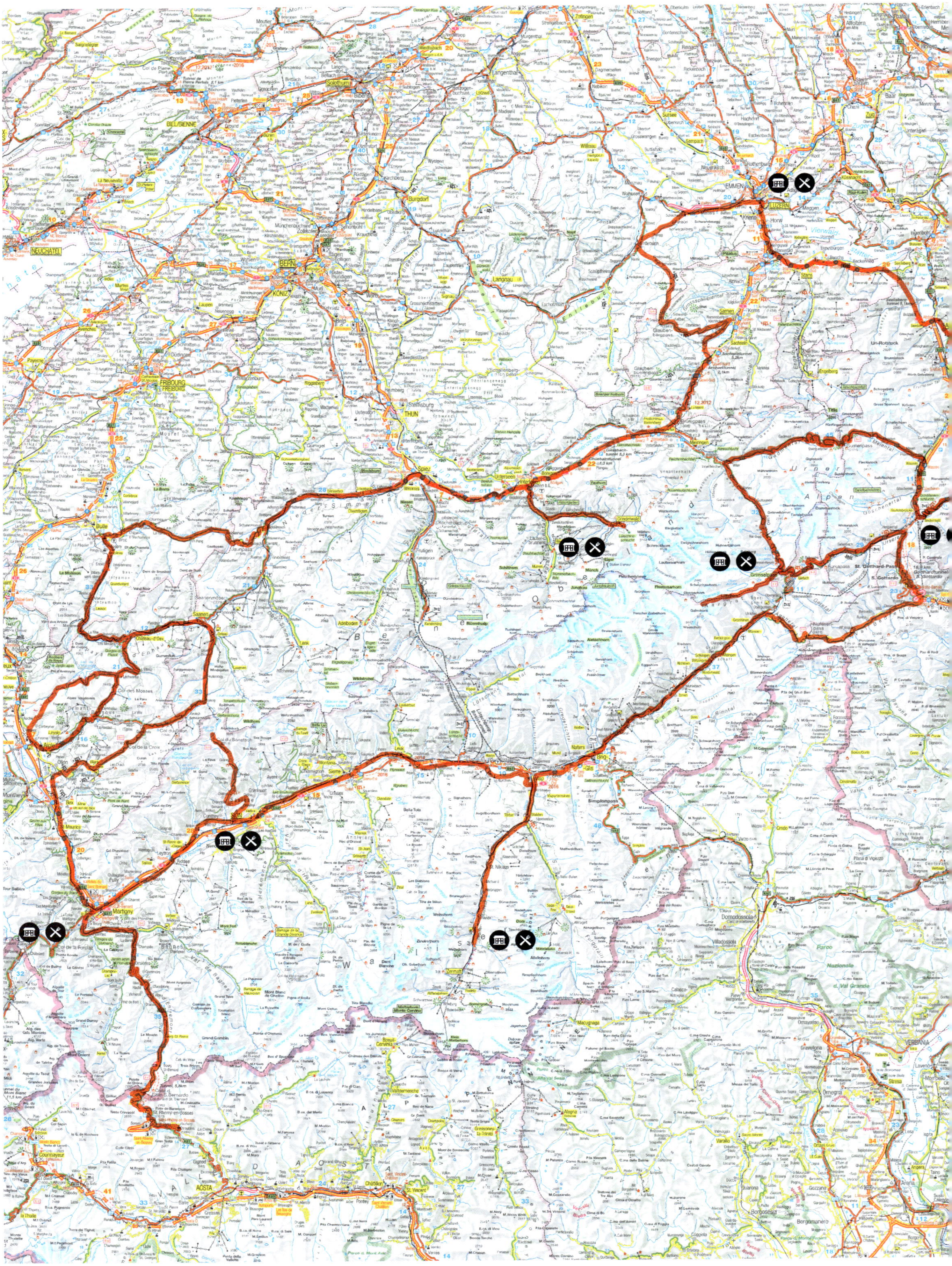

BIEL/BIENNE
NEUCHÂTEL
BERN
KÖNIZ
FRIBOURG
THUN
Burgdorf
Langnau
LUZERN
Emmen
Sarnen
Spiez
Interlaken
Brig
Sierre
Martigny
Zermatt
Domodossola
AOSTA
Courmayeur

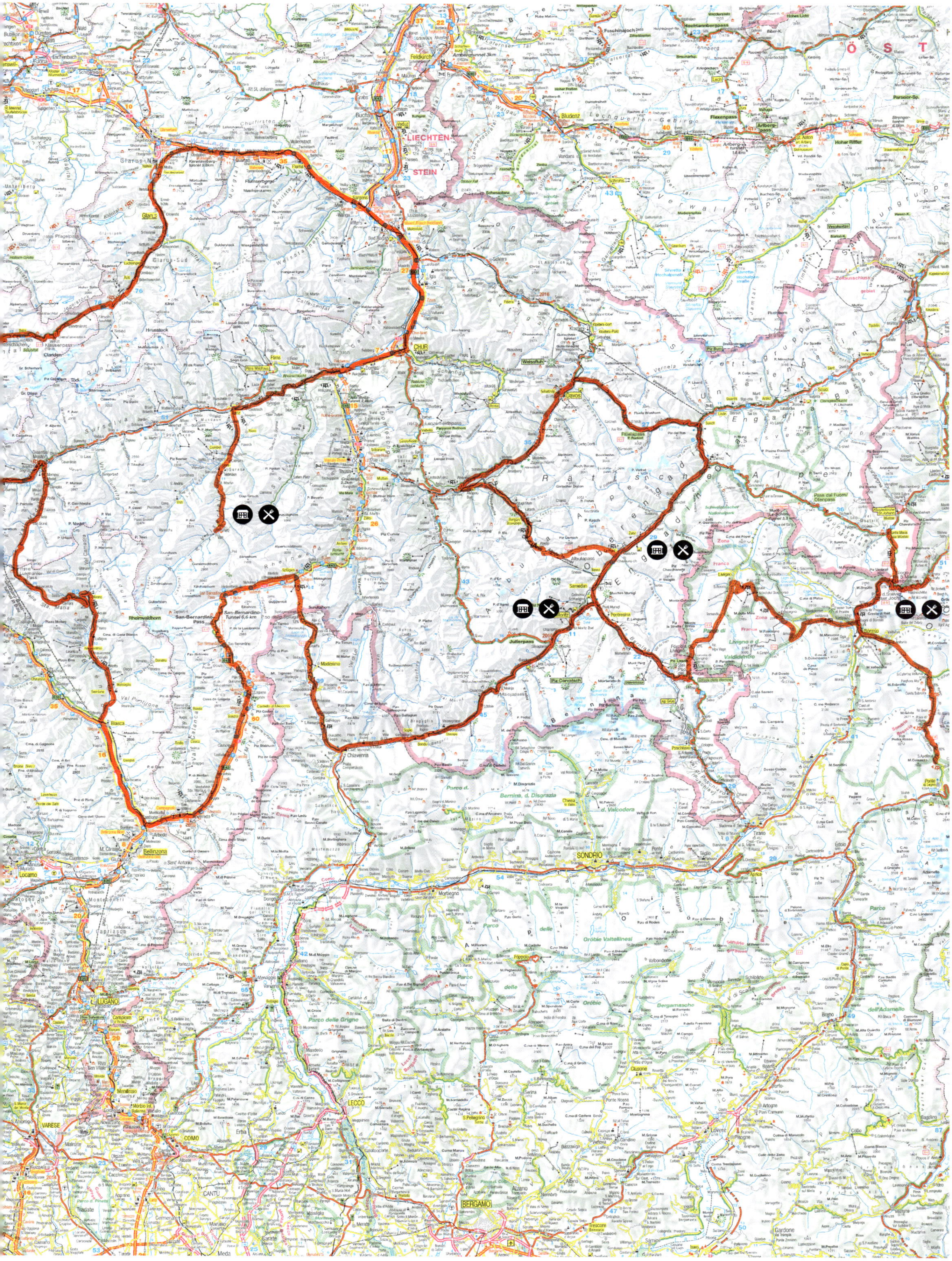

LIECHTEN
STEIN
CHUR
Davos
Feldkirch
Bludenz
Glarus
Flims
Samedan
Julierpass
Chiavenna
Bellinzona
Locarno
LUGANO
COMO
LECCO
SONDRIO
BERGAMO
VARESE
San-Bernardino-Pass
Tirano
Bormio
Livigno

GOTTHARDPASS

1 ETAPPE STAGE

Am östlichen Ende der Schweiz ist die Grenze turbulent. Österreich und Italien sind hier geschichtlich betrachtet keine klar abgesteckten Nachbarn, sondern haben sich entlang von Gebirgsketten und Tälern, unter dem Gerangel alter europäischer Adelshäuser bis in die Neuzeit ineinander verbissen. Es braucht also nicht viele Kilometer, um nach einem Start in die Schweiz hinein über den Umbrail-Pass geradewegs wieder das Land zu verlassen: Auf zum Stelvio-Pass, dem Stilfser Joch in Italien. Ohne eine Stippvisite zu diesem geschichtsträchtigen Kurvenwunder unter den Alpen-Pässen kann man eine Reise durch die Schweiz nicht angehen. Dann geht es aber nach Westen, über Bormio und einen zweiten Abstecher zum Gaviapass landen wir wieder in der Schweiz, direkt am Fuß des wilden Bernina-Pass, zwischen Poschiavo und Samedan. Zwischen Engadin und Veltlin. Zwischen allem was in Richtung Po-Ebene und Mittelmeer fließt und dem Wassersystem der Donau, die es bis zum Schwarzen Meer schaffen wird. Der Bernina ist nach dem heftigen Hakeln von Stelvio und Gavia ein flüssig zu fahrender Alpenpass, er bringt uns weiter in die Schweiz hinein. Nach einem weiteren Schwung über den Flüelapass und Albula-Pass sind wir zurück im Tal des hier noch sehr jungen Inn und beenden die Etappe in Sankt Moritz.

The border at the eastern end of Switzerland has had a turbulent history. In the past, Austria and Italy have not been the easiest of neighbors here, staking out their territories along the mountain ranges and valleys according to the age-old claims of Europe's aristocratic families until modern times. As a result it doesn't take long before you find yourself leaving Switzerland again via the Umbrail Pass: the Stelvio Pass takes you into Italy. No trip through Switzerland would be complete without a flying visit to this historic miracle among the region's curving Alpine passes. Our route then takes us west, via Bormio and a second detour to the Gavia Pass, when we arrive back in Switzerland, right at the foot of the wild Bernina Pass, between Poschiavo and Sameda, the Engadin and Valtellina. All the geological formations seem to flow towards the Po Valley and the Mediterranean and the great waterway of the Danube, which wends its way to the Black Sea. After the zig-zagging Stelvio and Gavia Passes, the Bernina affords a relatively smooth ride as it takes us further into Switzerland. Another hefty swing over the Flüela Pass and Albula-Pass takes us back to the valley of the River Inn, which is in its infancy here, and we end the stage in Sankt Moritz.

2 ETAPPE STAGE

Wir starten im Engadin, fahren von Sankt Moritz in Richtung der italienischen Grenze. Mit dem Malojapass grooven wir uns ein, schnuppern danach über Chiavenna in Richtung Splügenpass fahrend ein wenig italienisch-mediterranes Flair. Ein paar Kilometer später sollte man auf dieser Etappe so richtig warmgefahren sein, denn jetzt geht es über den San Bernardino, einen der großen Pass-Hauptdarsteller der Schweizer Alpen. In einer mächtigen Königsetappe führt uns der Sankt Bernhard, wie er auf Deutsch genannt wird, nach Süden. Wir verlassen Graubünden, fahren bei Bellinzona ins italienischsprachige Tessin und haben hier beinahe wieder den Norden Italiens erreicht. Mailand ist von hier nur noch ein Katzensprung. Wir schwenken dann aber wieder nach Norden ab, schließen uns mit dem Lukmanierpass wieder das Innere der Schweiz auf und landen erneut im rätoromanischen Graubünden. Über den Oberalppass geht es in den Kanton Uri, bei Andermatt haben wir das dramatische Finale dieser Tagesetappe erreicht: durch die Schöllenen-Schlucht ins Tal der Reuss – dann über den Sustenpass bis Innertkirchen im Kanton Bern. Und nun haben wir das Ziel endgültig vor Augen: die Fahrt hinauf zu den Stauseen am Grimselpass.

We start out in Engadin, travelling from Sankt Moritz toward the Italian border. We find our groove on the Maloja Pass, taking time to explore a little and passing through Chiavenna in the direction of the Splügen Pass and enjoying a little Italian Mediterranean flair. A few kilometers later and we've really hit our stride on this stage, traversing the San Bernardino Pass. This is one of the major passes in the Swiss Alps and certainly provides a majestic setting as it sweeps us south. We leave Graubünden, entering Italian-speaking Ticino at Bellinzona and finding ourselves once again within reach of northern Italy. Milan is just a stone's throw away. But then we swing north again, joining up with the Lukmanier Pass to dive back into Switzerland's interior and land again in Romansch territory in Graubünden. Crossing the Oberalp Pass to the Canton of Uri, near Andermatt we come to the dramatic finale of this day's stage: we make our way through the Schöllenen Gorge into the Reuss Valley, then over the Susten Pass to Innertkirchen in the canton of Bern. Finally we have our destination in our sights: the climb to the man-made lakes on the Grimsel Pass.

3 ETAPPE STAGE

Wir starten am 2.164 Meter hohen Grimselpass. Bevor wir aber nach Süden ins Tal der Rhône hineinrollen, legen wir einen landschaftlich sehr eindringlichen Abstecher zum Oberaargletscher ein. Die am Berghaus Oberaar endende Panoramastraße darf bei einer Grimsel-Überquerung eigentlich nicht fehlen. Bis hierher ist die Fahrt eindeutig schon atmosphärisch ungeheuer dicht, am Fuß des Grimselpasses angekommen, haben wir uns aber eine wahre Königsetappe erschlossen: Vorbei am Rhônegletscher nehmen wir den 2.429 Meter hohen Furkapass und sind nun direkt am legendären Gotthardpass (2.107 Meter) angelangt. Vor allem dessen Südflanke kann von leidenschaftlichen Kurven-Surfern unmöglich auf der neuen Asphalttrasse absolviert werden, eine Abfahrt nach Airolo über die traditionsreiche Kopfsteinpflaster-Route, der so genannten „Tremola", gehört beinahe zum Pflichtprogramm einer Alpenüberquerung. Mit dem 2.439 Meter hohen Nufenenpass gelangen wir ins oberste Stockwerk der Alpen, haben dann aber auch endgültig das Tor zu den Westalpen aufgestoßen. Abstecher nach Täsch – hier startet die Bahn ins autofrei Zermatt und damit zum Matterhorn –, nach Leukerbad oder zum Sanetschpass bei Sion gehören zum weiteren Verlauf dieser bemerkenswerten Alpen-Etappe, die in Martigny endet.

We start out on the 2,164-meter high Grimsel Pass. But before we head south into the Rhône valley, we first take an impressive scenic detour to the Oberaar Glacier. The panoramic route that ends at the Berghaus Oberaar hostel should not be missed when crossing the Grimsel Pass. Until now, the atmosphere on the journey has been extremely intense, but now, having arrived at the foot of the Grimsel Pass, we have entered a truly regal stage. Passing the Rhône Glacier, we take to the Furka Pass at 2,429 meters above sea level and find ourselves directly at the legendary Gotthard Pass (2,107 meters). Really passionate curve surfers will baulk at the idea of completing the southern side on the new asphalt route: a descent to Airolo via the traditional cobblestone route, the so-called "Tremola", is almost obligatory when crossing the Alps. At 2,439 meters above sea level, the Nufenen Pass takes us to the top of the Alps, finally opening the way to the Western Alps. A detour to Täsch where the train to car-free Zermatt and the Matterhorn departs, to Leukerbad or the Sanetsch Pass near Sion are part and parcel of this remarkable alpine stage, which ends in Martigny.

4 ETAPPE STAGE

Martigny liegt im Dreiländereck zwischen Schweiz, Italien und Frankreich. Hier, am beinahe südöstlichsten Punkt unserer Reise durch die Schweiz, fahren wir über den famosen Col de Champex bis zum Fuß des Grand Saint Bernard. Erst an der Passhöhe dieses 2.500 Meter hohen Bergpasses drehen wir mit einem Blick ins Aostatal ab. Der Weg führt uns zurück nach Martigny und dann weiter an der Rhône entlang in Richtung Genfersee. Abstecher in die angrenzenden Bergmassive von Les Diablerets oder zum Lac de l'Hongrin versüßen den Ritt nach Norden, in Richtung der Region Gruyère (Greyerz) streben wir dann weiter nach Norden. Lange Zeit bleiben wir im Tal der Saane und drehen dann nach Westen ab. Es geht nun über den Jaunpass bis ins Simmental, auf beinahe gerader Linie von West nach Ost. Nach dieser Fahrt durch die Kantone Wallis und Fribourg landen wir im Kanton Bern, hier erreichen wir nach vielen Kilometern im französischsprachigen Teil der Schweiz erneut die „schwyzerdütschen" Kantone. Von Spiez am Thunersee geht es nach Interlaken, hier muss ein Abstecher ins berühmte Grindelwald am Fuß der Eiger-Nordwand natürlich unbedingt sein. Nach einer Fahrt durch das UNESCO Biosphärenreservat Entlebuch erreichen wir in Luzern das Ziel der Etappe.

Martigny is located in the triangle between Switzerland, Italy and France. Here, at almost the most southerly point of our journey through Switzerland, we cross the famous Col de Champex to the foot of the Grand Saint Bernard. We wait until we reach the top of this 2,500 meter high mountain pass before turning to view the Aosta Valley. The path leads us back to Martigny and then further along the Rhône towards Lake Geneva. Detours to the nearby mountain massifs of Les Diablerets or to Lac de l'Hongrin are welcome rewards as we travel north toward the Gruyère region, after which we head further north again. We remain in the Saane valley for some time and then turn west. Then we cross the Jaun Pass to the Simmental Valley, following an almost straight line from west to east. After this trip through the cantons of Valais and Fribourg, we arrive in the canton of Bern, where, after many kilometers in the French-speaking part of Switzerland, we find ourselves once again in German-speaking territory. We travel from Spiez on Lake Thun to Interlaken, where we take a detour to the world-famous Grindelwald at the foot of the north face of the Eiger – a must. After a trip through the UNESCO World Heritage Site that is the Entlebuch Biosphere Reserve, we reach the end of this stage in Lucerne.

5 ETAPPE STAGE

Luzern ist eine Fahrpause wert, man muss es ganz klar sagen. Die Kantonshauptstadt im Westen des Vierwaldstättersees lockt mit einer sehenswerten Mischung aus neuzeitlicher Moderne und mittelalterlicher Atmosphäre, es gibt viel zu sehen. Für die Fahrt entlang des Vierwaldstättersees gilt das genauso: Der See liegt größtenteils so atemberaubend dicht ins Tal gepackt, dass die Straße sich entweder in gewundenen Felsgalerien und Tunnelpassagen wiederfindet oder überhaupt nicht direkt ans Seeufer gelangt. Gelegentlich wirkt das beinahe wie ein skandinavischer Fjord, die vielen Nebentäler und Windungen des großen Sees tragen zusätzlich zur magischen Stimmung bei. Gleichzeitig ballt sich Schweizer Geschichte rund um den See – wer hier etwas Hintergrundwissen gesammelt hat, fährt auch noch durch eine unsichtbare Wolke von eidgenössischen Legenden. Über den Klausenpass verlassen wir die Gegend um den Vierwaldstättersee in östlicher Richtung, die Fahrt ins Tal der Linth streckt sich weit und dauert ohne Pausen bereits rund eine Stunde. Über Glarus stoßen wir dann weiter bis zum Walensee vor, rollen in herrlicher Panoramalage entlang des Südufers nach Osten und auf Sargans zu. Hier, im Rheintal, sollten Heidi-Fans unbedingt einen Abstecher in die Gegend um Maienfeld und Bad Ragaz unternehmen, für alle anderen geht es den Flusslauf hinauf über Chur bis Reichenau. Mit dem Vorderrhein erreichen wir Ilanz und fahren dann dem Etappenende bei Vals entgegen.

We must admit that it is worth taking a break from driving to explore Lucerne. The cantonal capital in the western part of Lake Lucerne attracts visitors for its mixture of modernity and medieval atmosphere. It is certainly well worth as visit as there is so much to see. The same is true of the drive along Lake Lucerne: the lake is for the most part packed so tightly into the valley that the road either follows winding rock galleries and tunnels or remains a long way from the lakeshore. Occasionally it almost looks like a Scandinavian fjord, the many side valleys and winding inlets of the huge lake adding to the magical atmosphere. Switzerland's history is also concentrated around the lake and, armed with a little background knowledge, you can find yourself driving through an invisible cloud of Swiss legends. We leave the area around Lake Lucerne in an easterly direction via the Klausen Pass. The journey into the Linth Valley is a long one and takes around an hour without stops. We then move on via Glarus to Lake Walen, where we follow a wonderful panoramic route along the south bank to the east towards Sargans. Here, in the Rhine Valley, Heidi fans should definitely take a detour to the area around Maienfeld and Bad Ragaz. Everyone else should head up river via Chur to Reichenau. Joining the Vorderrhein, we reach Ilanz and then drive to the end of the stage in Vals.

EDITORIAL

Autokennzeichen CH. Confoederatio Helvetica. Allein der Name dieses Landes ist gelebter Kompromiss. Eine Konföderation ist die Schweiz nämlich nicht: Ihre Kantone haben politisch betrachtet zwar eine große Schippe Eigenständigkeit und Souveränität, tatsächliche Staaten, die sich lediglich in einer konföderierten Dachorganisation zusammengeschlossen hätten, sind sie aber keineswegs. Die plakative Andeutung echter Souveränität darf also dem Selbstbewusstsein der Kantone schmeicheln, korrekt ist sie allerdings nicht. Und dann dieses zweite Wort: Helvetica. Den Kelten-Stamm der Helvetier gibt es schon lange nicht mehr, er hat sich im diffusen Nebel grauer Vorzeit den germanisch-alemannischen Stämmen der Alpenregionen angeschlossen. Als aber im wachsenden Zweckbündnis dieser vielkulturellen Gruppen ein gemeinsamer Name gesucht war, der keinen Kanton, keine Sprache der Schweiz bevorzugte, griff man in einem wahren Geniestreich auf den alten Stammesnamen der Helvetier zurück. Ein untergegangenes Volk als Namensgeber eines Staates, darauf muss man kommen. Genau das ist typisch für die Schweiz: konsequenter Kompromiss.

Mit vier offiziellen Amtssprachen – Deutsch, Französisch, Italienisch und Rätoromanisch – sowie mindestens ebenso vielen Kulturen kommt die Schweiz ganz elegant zurecht. Egal, ob es das lockere Laissez-faire der französischsprachigen Romandie ist, das lebensfroh-mediterrane des italienischsprachigen Tessins, das puritanisch-korrekte der deutschsprachigen Kantone in der Zentral- und Nordschweiz oder die eigenwillige Gelassenheit der rätoromanischen Kantone – die Schweiz bekommt das alles unter einen Hut. Weil sie nicht nur nach außen strikt und sprichwörtlich neutral ist, sondern vor allem nach innen. Der Ausgleich gehört zu ihrer DNA, nicht die kulturelle Identität. In diesem Klima entstehen keine Leitkulturen, sondern es bleibt Raum für Individualität und Minderheiten, fürs Leben und leben lassen. Und jetzt darf man das ganz bestimmt nicht als laxe Liberalität missverstehen: Vor

Switzerland's car license plates carry the letters CH for Confoederatio Helvetica. The very name of this country is a compromise. After all, Switzerland is not really a confederation. From a political perspective, its cantons enjoy a great deal of independence and sovereignty, but are by no means actual states that have simply come together under a federal umbrella. The suggestion of genuine sovereignty may flatter the self-esteem of the cantons, but it is essentially incorrect. And then there's the second word: Helvetica. The Celtic tribe of the Helvetii has long ceased to exist, having merged with the Germanic-Alemannic tribes of the Alpine regions in the gray mists of prehistoric times. However, as the alliance between these multicultural groups began to flourish and needed a common name that did not favor any particular canton or language in Switzerland, people fell on the old tribal name of the Helvetii in a true stroke of genius. Choosing a lost people as namesake for a state is an idea that needs time to mature. This is typical for Switzerland: consistent compromise.

Switzerland manages very elegantly with four official languages – German, French, Italian and Romansh – as well as at least as many cultures. From the laid-back laissez-faire of French-speaking Romandy, the cheerful Mediterranean temperament of Italian-speaking Ticino, the puritanical correctness of the German-speaking cantons in central and northern Switzerland or the idiosyncratic serenity of the Romansch cantons, Switzerland succeeds in bringing a host of divergent characteristics under one roof. That's because it is not only strictly and literally neutral on the outside, but, significantly, also on the inside. This balance is part of the Swiss DNA, if not its cultural identity. No particular culture is allowed to take the lead here, but instead space is created for individuality and minorities. Live and let live is the motto. This should definitely not be misunderstood as laisser-faire liberalism: after all, the German-speaking Swiss, who rightly regard themselves as the

allem die deutschsprachigen Schweizer, die sich als Gründer der Eidgenossenschaft betrachten dürfen, sind streit- und wehrhaft, man pocht auf Gemeinsinn und Ordnung – weil es gerade diese Attribute sind, die am Ende der turbulenten Mischung eine Fassung und Form verleihen. Individuelle Freiheit hat in der Schweiz einen hohen Wert, aber auch klar abgesteckte Grenzen: Sie endet exakt dort, wo die des Nachbarn beginnt.

Freiheit misst man in der Schweiz also in Qualität, nicht in Quantität, diese Maxime erlebt der Schweiz-Reisende gern einmal bereits auf den ersten Kilometern nach der Fahrt über die Grenze, wenn knackscharfe Fotos der Verkehrsüberwachung mit schwindelerregenden Bußgeldern garniert an die akribisch überwachten Tempolimits erinnern. Sei gern, wer du bist, aber halt dich an die Regeln aller – das ist die vollkommen unmissverständliche Botschaft. Die Lernkurve der Undisziplin ist vor diesem Hintergrund außerordentlich steil. Es dauert selten länger als zwei bemerkenswert schmerzhafte Blitz-Auslösungen, bis selbst der freiheitsliebendste Tempo-Ritter seine Gangart nachhaltig ändert, vom kernigen Fast-Forward-Modus in gelassenen und umsichtigen Flow wechselt – und dann feststellt, dass Geschwindigkeit keine Mindestvoraussetzung für intensives Auto- oder Motorradfahren ist. Sondern eher das Soulful Driving.

Auch in dieser Hinsicht fühlt sich CURVES in der Schweiz ungemein wohl, das Land hat genau unseren Groove. Und die Schweizer trotz eines nicht verhandelbaren Verkehrsregelwerks eine ausgelassene Freude am Fahren, am Automobil, am Reisen. Es sind die himmelhochjauchzenden Passstraßen der Schweiz, die seit Generationen Automobilisten und Motorrad-Windgesichter aus ganz Europa anlocken. Magische Routen über die Berge, die durch ihre Landschaften und Streckenführung innere Saiten anschlagen, sie singen und klingen lassen. Man kommt aus den Bergen nicht wieder so nach Hause wie man in sie hineingefahren ist. Und es darf auch gesagt sein: Ohne uns, die Soulful Drivers, wäre die Schweiz nicht, was sie ist. Nur die alpinen Sportarten haben einen noch prägenderen Eindruck hinterlassen, dann kommen auch schon die Reisenden auf ihrer „Gran Tour", die auf ihren traumwandlerischen Wegen über das Gebirge Straßen und Hotels, Gaststätten und Trassen haben blühen lassen. Mit dieser Feststellung hätten wir die lange, erklärende Anreise ins Innere der Schweiz hinter uns. Wir sind über die ersten Gebirgsketten

founders of the Confederation, can be a pretty pugnacious and defensive lot. They insist on civic-mindedness and order – because these are precisely the attributes that lend sense and shape to this turbulent ethnic mixture. Individual freedom has a high value in Switzerland, but also clearly defined boundaries, ending precisely our neighbor's garden fence.

Freedom is something the Swiss measure in terms of quality, not quantity. Travelers in Switzerland will experience this fact for themselves just a few kilometers after they have crossed the border, when stark traffic surveillance photos, accompanied by a list of head-spinning fines, provide a reminder of the meticulously monitored speed limits. The unmistakable message is: you're welcome to be as free as you like, but everyone has to stick to the rules. The learning curve for undisciplined types can be extraordinarily steep in this context. It rarely takes more than two painful flashes of the speed cameras before even the most freedom-loving knight of the road slows his pace from robust high-speed mode to calm and prudent flow. This is accompanied by the realization that speed is not a minimum requirement for an intense driving or motorbike experience. It's more about soulful driving.

This is also why CURVES feels extremely at home in Switzerland. The country really suits our groove. Furthermore the Swiss, despite a non-negotiable set of traffic regulations, really enjoy driving and adore their automobiles and the chance to travel. Switzerland's sky-high mountain pass roads have been attracting motorists and motorcyclists from all over Europe for generations. These magical routes through the mountains pluck at our heart strings, making them vibrate and sing. You return home from the mountains a different person from when you drove into them. You might also say that Switzerland would not be what it is today without soulful drivers like us. Other than alpine sports, few things have made an even deeper impression on the country than the travelers on the "Grand Tour", who have helped highways and hotels, restaurants and routes blossom on the paths of dreams over the mountains. In coming to this conclusion, we have completed the long, journey of the mind into the beating heart of Switzerland. We have crossed the first mountain ranges of the understanding, and are now moving as if in a hypnotic and powerful dream. The end of this imaginative journey marks the

des Verstehens gefahren, und nun wie im Traum unterwegs, hypnotisch und mächtig. Das Ende der Anreise ist der Beginn der eigentlichen Fahrt: durch die Schweiz, dieses altbekannte, immer wieder fremde und so vielfältige Land in der Mitte Europas, das in jeder Hinsicht eine Berg- und Talfahrt ist. Wir können an dieser Stelle nur eines raten: Mach dich locker. Lass dich von der Schweiz überraschen, sie wird dir das früher oder später ohnehin beibringen. Hier ist die Welt unter einer knusprig-dünnen Oberfläche unfassbar tief. Geschichten stehen wie dichter Nebel in einer magischen Landschaft, unsichtbar, aber du spürst ihre Vibrationen. Die Schweiz, das ist Infraschall-Storytelling. Jahrhundertealte Nanometer-Krustenbildung aus Geschichte, die kilometerhohe Riffe hinterlässt – gut erkennbar, wenn man nur hinsieht.

Dieses Land ist heute bemerkenswert altmodisch, es lässt sich von der Hetze des Zeitgeists nicht aus der Ruhe bringen. Traditionen werden gut und natürlich gelebt, eine selbstbewusste Imprägnierung gegen die Abnutzungserscheinungen moderner Beliebigkeit gehören untrennbar zur Schweiz. Das darf allerdings nicht mit bockiger oder gar verzweifelter Gestrigkeit verwechselt werden, ganz bestimmt nicht. Denn Dynamik und Aktion sind ganz genauso sehr ein Elixier der Schweiz. Die immer wieder durchgeführten Volksentscheide sind ein gutes Beispiel dafür: Im einen Moment bekennen sich die Schweizer Bürger zu knochentrockenem Konservativismus und beim nächsten Entscheid stimmen sie für bemerkenswerte Modernität, gehen nicht nur mit der Zeit, sondern sind ihr sogar den einen oder anderen Schritt voraus. Genau so geht das auch in Wirtschaft und Industrie, Leben und Gesellschaft: Humorloser Pragmatismus meets Lebensfreude, eiserne Grundsätze schunkeln mit verblüffender Agilität.

All das sei nur dahingeworfen, damit der Reisende dieses Land ein wenig besser einschätzen kann, es ist immer für eine Überraschung gut. Aber am Ende wollten wir doch einfach nur hoch hinauf

beginning of the actual journey: through Switzerland. The country feels familiar yet always foreign. Its diversity makes it a real central European roller-coaster ride in every respect. We can only offer one piece of advice at this point: relax and let Switzerland surprise you. Sooner or later that's going to happen anyway. This is a world of incredible hidden depths beneath a brittle, wafer-thin surface. Invisible stories swirl like thick fog around this magical landscape. You can feel them vibrate as Switzerland whispers to your soul. Centuries of history are framed by towering mountain peaks, leaving clues to the past that are easily recognizable if you just look closely enough.

This is a curiously old-fashioned country. It doesn't allow itself to get over-excited by the latest, fast-moving trends. Traditions are honored in a positive and natural way, making the Swiss self-consciously impervious to the transient and random fads that are a feature of modern life elsewhere. However, this shouldn't be confused with stubbornness or even a desperate clinging to the past. After all, dynamism and action are just as much part of the Swiss character. The country's frequently-held plebiscites are a good example of this: one moment the Swiss people seem to commit themselves to bone-dry conservatism and the next they vote for something remarkably modern, not only moving with the times, but sometimes one step ahead.

It's exactly the same in business and industry, life and society: humorless pragmatism meets joie de vivre, iron-clad principles can change with astonishing agility. Travelers need to cast all of these thoughts aside in order to understand this country a little better. Switzerland always has a surprise up its sleeve. But in the end all we wanted was a trip up to the San Bernardino Pass and over the Gotthard, Klausen or Nufenen Pass. We're like junkies when it comes to curves and space, addicted to drifting. Switzerland is the perfect place for this attitude to life. The mountains and the spirits that live there don't make things easy for you, so you have to fight your way forward.

Die Berge und ihre Geister machen es einem nicht leicht, man muss sich den Weg erkämpfen. Und um diese Reibung geht es, man wird sie nach der ersten Fahrt durch die Schweiz immer wieder suchen.

auf den San Bernardino, über den Gotthard, den Klausen- oder Nufenenpass. Wir sind Nomaden der Kurven und der Weite, dem Dahinziehen verfallen. Für dieses Lebensgefühl ist die Schweiz Heimat und Zuhause. Die Berge und ihre Geister machen es einem nicht leicht, man muss sich den Weg erkämpfen. Und um diese Reibung geht es, man wird sie nach der ersten Fahrt durch die Schweiz immer wieder suchen. Allein ihre ungeheure Vielfalt auf wirklich überschaubarem Raum ist ein wesentlicher Charakterzug der Schweiz und man findet sie nicht nur in den Kulturen und Menschen, sondern auch in den Landschaften. Wer einmal im Winter von Nord nach Süd gefahren ist, im einen Tal klirrende Temperaturen um den Gefrierpunkt und im nächsten Tal frühsommerliches T-Shirt-Wetter bei Fön erlebt hat, muss immer wieder an diese kleinen, schnellen Taschenspielertricks der Alpen denken. Zumeist funktioniert die Schweiz aber in längeren Spannungsbögen. Ihre Landschaften erzählen viele Kapitel mit unzähligen Wendungen.

In diesem CURVES fahren wir von Osten herkommend hinein, tasten uns mit offenen Sinnen ins sonnige, liebliche Engadin, unter dessen freundlicher Oberfläche sich aber eine große Komplexität verbirgt. Dann geht es weiter über die mächtigen Gebirgspässe, diese düsteren Gesellen mit großem Hang zur Dramatik, und schließlich weiter ins blumige, saftige und sinnliche Tessin. Um dieses Erlebnis zu konterkarieren, rollen wir im Tal der Rhône nach Südwesten, erleben eine Schweiz, die offen und alltäglich ist, den eleganten Charme französischer Lebensart pflegt. Von dort geht es in ländliche Welten, rustikal, gottesfürchtig – und unter der Oberfläche hausen heidnische Kobolde, die einen kichernd und mit bösen Scherzen in die Zentralschweiz hinüberjagen. Zu den Seen und Mythen in ein Land, das man beinahe in eine gläserne Diorama-Schneekugel stecken und lächelnd schütteln würde, wenn es sich einem nicht mit seiner Wildheit und Schroffheit gleich wieder entziehen würde. Die Schweiz, das ist eine ganze, herrliche Welt im Taschenformat. Wir lieben sie. Und Sie bald auch. Wetten?

The mountains and the spirits that live there don't make things easy for you, so you have to fight your way forward. This friction is the key: you'll encounter it again and again after your first trip through Switzerland.

This friction is the key: you'll encounter it again and again after your first trip through Switzerland. The country's immense diversity in a really compact space is an essential characteristic and is found not only in the cultures and people, but also in the landscapes. If you have ever driven through Switzerland from north to south in winter, experiencing freezing temperatures in one valley and early summer conditions in the next, you'll never forget the tiny sleight-of-hand tricks played by the Alps. For the most part, however, Switzerland is all about lengthy narrative arcs, with landscapes that tell innumerable tales with countless twists and turns.

In this edition of CURVES we will be approaching from the east, opening our senses to the country's sunny side in Engadin, a region whose friendly disposition can hide a complex character. We then drive onward to the mighty mountain passes, their saturnine personalities betraying a great penchant for melodrama, and finally moving on to flowery, juicy and sensual Ticino. As a balance to this experience, we head southwest through the valley of the Rhône, experiencing a more open, everyday aspect of the country with the cultivated, elegant charm of the French way of life. From there we plunge into a rural, god-fearing world, where pagan goblins lurk just below the surface, waiting to chase you into Central Switzerland in a cackling flurry of bad jokes. We encounter lakes and legends in a country that is almost small enough to put inside a snow globe and shake with a smile, were it not for its wild ruggedness. Switzerland is an entire world, but pocket-sized. We love it. We bet you will too. Ready to gamble?

SAN BERNHARDINO

GOTTHARDPASS

GRIMSELPASS

SUSTENPASS

BERNINAPASS

ALETSCHGLETSCHER

HOTEL
GLETSCHER - RESTAURANT
BELVEDERE

ALBULAPASS

SUSTENPASS

FLÜELAPASS

GOTTHARDPASS

FURKAPASS

GRIMSELPASS

GRIMSELPASS

MÜSTAIR
ST. MORITZ

320 KM • 6 STUNDEN // 198 MILES • 6 HOURS

Val Müstair, Münstertal. Das ist hinter den Bergen. Tief im saftigen, herben Inneren der Alpen. Man kann einfach unbekümmert hineinfahren ins Tal und im Rückspiegel zusehen, wie waldbedeckte Berge mit Fels-Tonsur unter einem azurblauen Sommerberghimmel in den grasgrünen Talboden sinken. Aber höchstens bis zum Benediktinerinnenkloster Sankt Johann, das hier an der Grenze bei Taufers den Eingang in die Schweiz bewacht.

—

Val Müstair: the land beyond the mountains. We penetrate deep into the lush, yet harsh interior of the Alps. You can blithely sail into the valley without a care in the world, watching in your rear-view mirror as bald mountain peaks become tree-covered slopes before finally dissolving into the grass-green valley floor under an azure blue summer sky. But things change when you catch sight of the Benedictine monastery of Sankt Johann, which guards the gateway to Switzerland here on the border near Taufers.

UMBRAILPASS

Hospiz
St. Bernhardin
GASTHAUS RESTAURANT

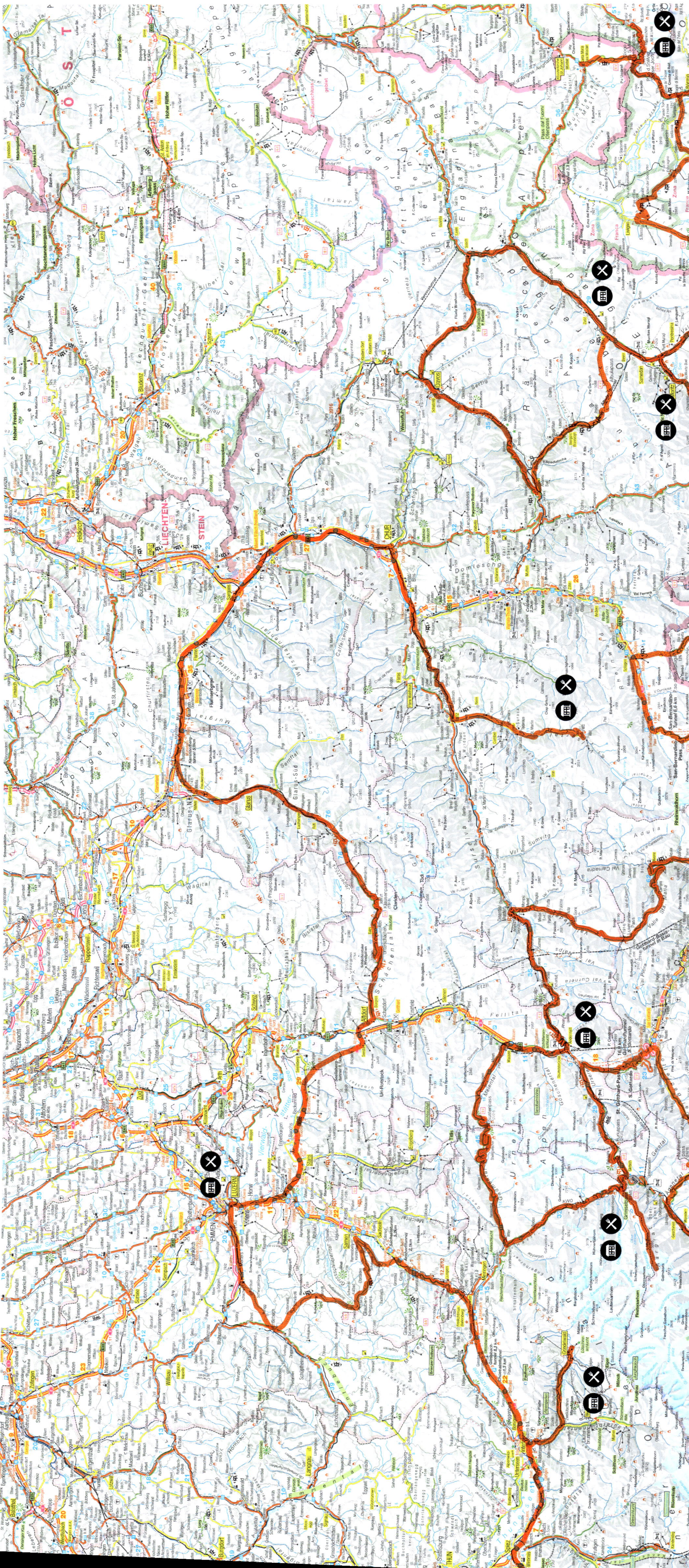

CURVES
MAGAZIN EST. 2011
soulful driving

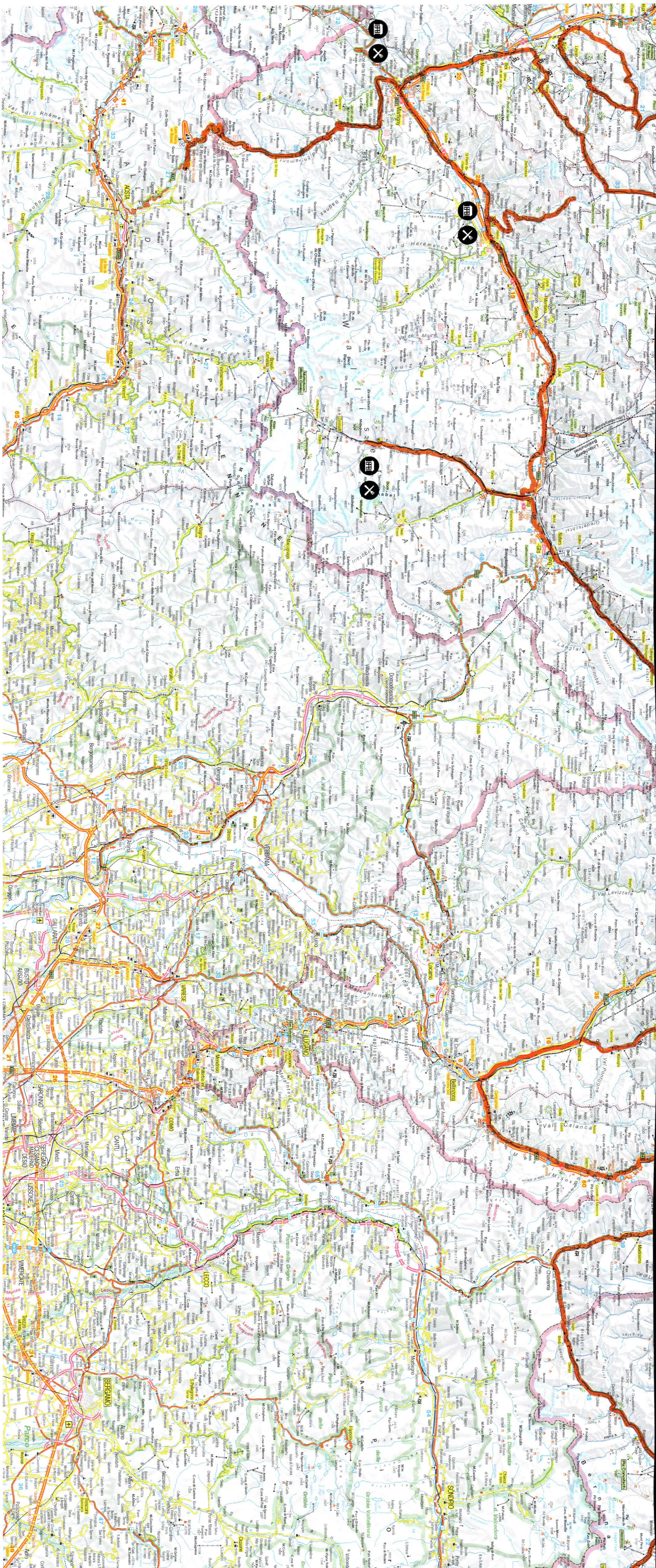

Blanke, kalkweiße Mauern strammstehen lässt, misstrauisch aus vielen Fenstern herüber zur Straße schaut, während ein Sommertag beschwichtigend zwischen den Mauerzinnen tanzt. Das Frühmittelalter hat gern solche Gebäude hinterlassen, roh und klotzig, argwöhnisch und karg – man scheint das Leben damals nicht als Spaß verstanden zu haben. Das macht heute noch etwas mit dem vorüberströmenden Reisenden, der unwillkürlich das Autoradio herunterdreht, das Schnattern sein lässt und dann auf gefühlten Zehenspitzen vorbeihuscht, während einen Moment lang steinkalter Hauch des 8. Jahrhunderts aus der Heiligkreuzkapelle herüberweht.

Dann ist der Moment auch schon wieder vorbei, die Straße huscht erleichtert das Tal hinauf. Bunte Lupinen drängen sich an Gartenzäunen und lassen sich von einem lauwarmen Wind die Blüten zerzausen. In Santa Maria wohnen Geranien in mächtigen Steinhäusern und haben Menschen zur Untermiete akzeptiert. Rattattatternde Kehrtwende in Kopfsteinpflaster-Seitengassen, weil wir die Auffahrt mitten im Ort in Richtung Stelvio verpasst haben – dann sind wir auf Kurs und an der Bergflanke unterwegs. Mit ausgelassenem Schwung kurvt die Straße aus dem Tal hinauf, nimmt die ersten Serpentinen übereifrig und gleich mehrere auf einmal, dann hat sie ihren Rhythmus gefunden. Gerade, zwo, drei, vier, ein Serpentinen-Akkord und dann wieder Gerade. So geht der Umbrail-Pass, während er vom sattgrünen Talboden bis zu seiner Passhöhe groovt. Dort geht uns die Schweiz bereits wieder aus, an der Ecke beim arg gebeutelten Casa Cantoniera dello Stelvio beginnt Italien wieder.

Dass wir an der Umbrail-Passhöhe dann nicht der Straße nach Westen folgen – dort wäre nämlich die Schweiz wiederzufinden –, sondern vollends zum Stelvio hinauffahren, ist keine Überraschung. Man kommt an dieser Ecke der Welt nicht vorbei, ohne zum Stilfser Joch hinaufzusurfen. Man muss da oben dann nur aufpassen, dass einen Schwung und Begeisterung nicht auf der anderen Seite wieder hinuntertragen. Vor allem, weil die harten, steilen Kehren der Stelvio-Ostrampe ja die eigentliche Attraktion des Passes sind. Und deshalb kehren wir jetzt um, fahren... wie? Sie nicht? Schon weg?

Bare, chalk-white walls stand to attention, while empty windows gaze suspiciously down at the road below and the brilliant light of a summer's day dances skittishly between the battlements. The master-builders of the early Middle Ages certainly liked make their mark on the landscape, creating spare, unwelcoming hulks that seem to stifle any sense of joy in life. The effect still lingers today, as passing travelers instinctively turn down the car radio, falling silent for a few moments and slipping past almost on tiptoe, while a stone-cold breath of wind from the 8th century wafts from the Chapel of the Holy Cross.

The moment passes and the road scrambles up the valley with a sigh of relief. Brightly colored lupines crowd against garden fences and a warm breeze ruffles the flower heads. The geraniums in Santa Maria have made themselves completely at home in the mighty stone houses and seem to have grudgingly accepted the presence of human beings as temporary fellow-tenants. We make a bone-shaking U-turn in one of the cobblestoned side streets, having missed the road for Stelvio in the middle of the village. Finally we find ourselves on course and start the mountain climb. The road curves up from the valley in an exuberant gesture, betraying over-excitement on the first of several hairpin bends before finally finding its rhythm. Straight ... two, three, four ... twist, two, three, four ... then straight again. That's what you can expect from the Umbrail Pass, as it carves a path from the saturated colors of the green valley floor to the dizzying heights of the pass itself. We leave Switzerland behind and are in Italy once again as we round the corner of the battle-scarred Casa Cantoniera dello Stelvio.

It comes as little surprise to find that we are not following the road to the west at the summit of the Umbrail Pass – after all this would take us back into Switzerland. Instead we inevitably climb all the way up to the Stelvio Pass, a must for any drive in this part of the world. Once you reach the top, you just have to take care not to get carried away in your enthusiasm, allowing your momentum to send you careering down the other side. The sharp, steep bends on the Stelvio's east side are the main attraction here. That's why we're going to turn back at this point ...

HOTELS

BERGHOTEL FRANZENSHÖHE
VIA DEL PASSO, 47
39029 TRAFOI BZ
WWW.FRANZENSHOEHE.COM

HOTEL BELLA VISTA
VIA TRAFOI, 11
39029 STELVIO BZ
WWW.BELLA-VISTA.IT

CHASA CHALAVAINA
PLAZ GROND 24
7537 MÜSTAIR

IMBISS

RICHARD RITSCH
WÜRSTELSTAND

129

Runter zur Franzenshöhe? Sogar noch weiter bis Trafoi? – Also gut, wir verstehen Sie ja. Eine knappe Stunde später werden Sie abgehetzt und mit leuchtenden Augen zurück am Stelvio sein, wir fahren dann zufrieden zurück zur Umbrail-Passhöhe und rodeln weiter der Strada Statale 38 folgend den Berg hinunter, nach Südwesten. Ein paar Rennradfahrer sind jetzt mit uns unterwegs, tief über die Lenker geduckt und mit Fahrtwind-Freudentränen auf den Wangen. Dünne Leibchen flattern, rasierte Stahlwaden holen auf den wenigen Bergabgeraden noch das Letzte an Speed heraus, dann werfen sie vor den wüsten Serpentinen am Fuß des Monte Radisca doch mit flatternden Rahmen das Handtuch und gehen vom Gas. Wir grüßen im Vorbeifahren beeindruckt: Ave Gladiatores Pedales. Eines hat sich jetzt aber herausgestellt:

Nicht der berühmte Osten des Stelvio-Passes ist seine Schokoladenseite, sondern die Westrampe. Verdammt, geht das ab. Völlige innere Verwahrlosung macht sich breit, die Sitten verrohen, du wirst zur Bergabdampfwalze, zum Fahrspaß-Hammer, lässt die Lefzen flattern und genießt den Ritt. Erst in Bormio ist alles vorbei, mit weichen Knien und freudestrahlend landen wir in der Zivilisation. – Der Entzug schlägt hart zu. Aber da wäre ja noch ein zweiter Abstecher machbar. Hinunter nach Santa Catarina und den Gaviapass hinauf. Der tummelt sich so herrlich am Übergang in die Region Brescia, dass man ihn gern als weitere Perle am Rosenkranz dieser Fahrt durch die Finger gleiten lässt. Knackige Serpentinen im unteren Drittel und dann über die schmale Straße in den weiten Bergrampen zum Sattel. Der Gaviapass ist uralt, seine Route dürfte schon hier verlaufen sein, als Räder noch nicht erfunden waren, ganz abgesehen von Straßen – und selbst in die Neuzeit hat er es nur geschafft, weil man ihn im Ersten Weltkrieg als strategisch zielführend betrachtet hat. Aber das ist eine andere Geschichte.

Wir fahren zurück. Bis nach Bormio, dann entlang des Flusses Adda in westlicher Richtung. Das Tal steigt an, Bergketten schließen uns ein, schneebedeckte Gipfel warten auf uns: Hier kommst du nicht so einfach wieder heraus. Aber die Straße lässt sich nicht einschüchtern, zieht ihr Ding durch und tapfer voran. Schraubt sich taktisch klug

What's that? You're continuing on? Looks like you're already on your way down to Franzenshöhe? And then on to Trafoi? - All right, we get it. It takes less than an hour before we see you back at the Stelvio Pass, your eyes burning bright and your body exhausted. Satisfied, we happily drive back to the Umbrail pass and continue to hurtle down the mountain along Strada Statale 38, heading southwest. By now a couple of racing cyclists have joined us on the road, hunched low over the handlebars and tears of joy running down their cheeks from the biting wind. Their thin cycling vests flutter wildly as their muscular, steely calves extract the last bit of speed from the wheels on the few downhill straights. Finally they concede the race, slowing down before reaching the harsh hairpin bends at the foot of Monte Radisca. We salute their efforts with a suitable Latin phrase as we drive past: Ave gladiatores pedales.

One thing has now become clear: the famous east side of the Stelvio Pass is not the real gem – the west side is far better. Boy, is it a fast ride! You lose all sense of decorum and forget your manners entirely as you power down the mountainside like a pile driver, your lips distorting under the force of the air on your face as you enjoy the ride. And so it goes on until we reach civilization in Bormio, all beaming smiles and legs like jelly. The withdrawal symptoms hit us hard, making a second detour almost irresistible. We decide to try the descent to Santa Catarina, followed by a climb up the Gavia Pass. Driving is so wonderful here at the border with the Brescia region that this feels like just another beautiful link on the precious necklace that is this road trip.

We negotiate crisp serpentine bends on the lower third of the descent and then follow the narrow road up the broad mountain slopes to reach the saddle. The Gavia Pass is an ancient route and was already in use before the invention of the wheel, not to mention roads. Even in more recent times a road was only built here because it was considered of strategic benefit in the First World War. But that's another story. We make the return journey, driving as far as Bormio, then along the River Adda heading west. The valley start to rise and mountains envelop us on either side, their now-capped peaks beckoning us onward: it won't be easy to escape

GAVIAPASS

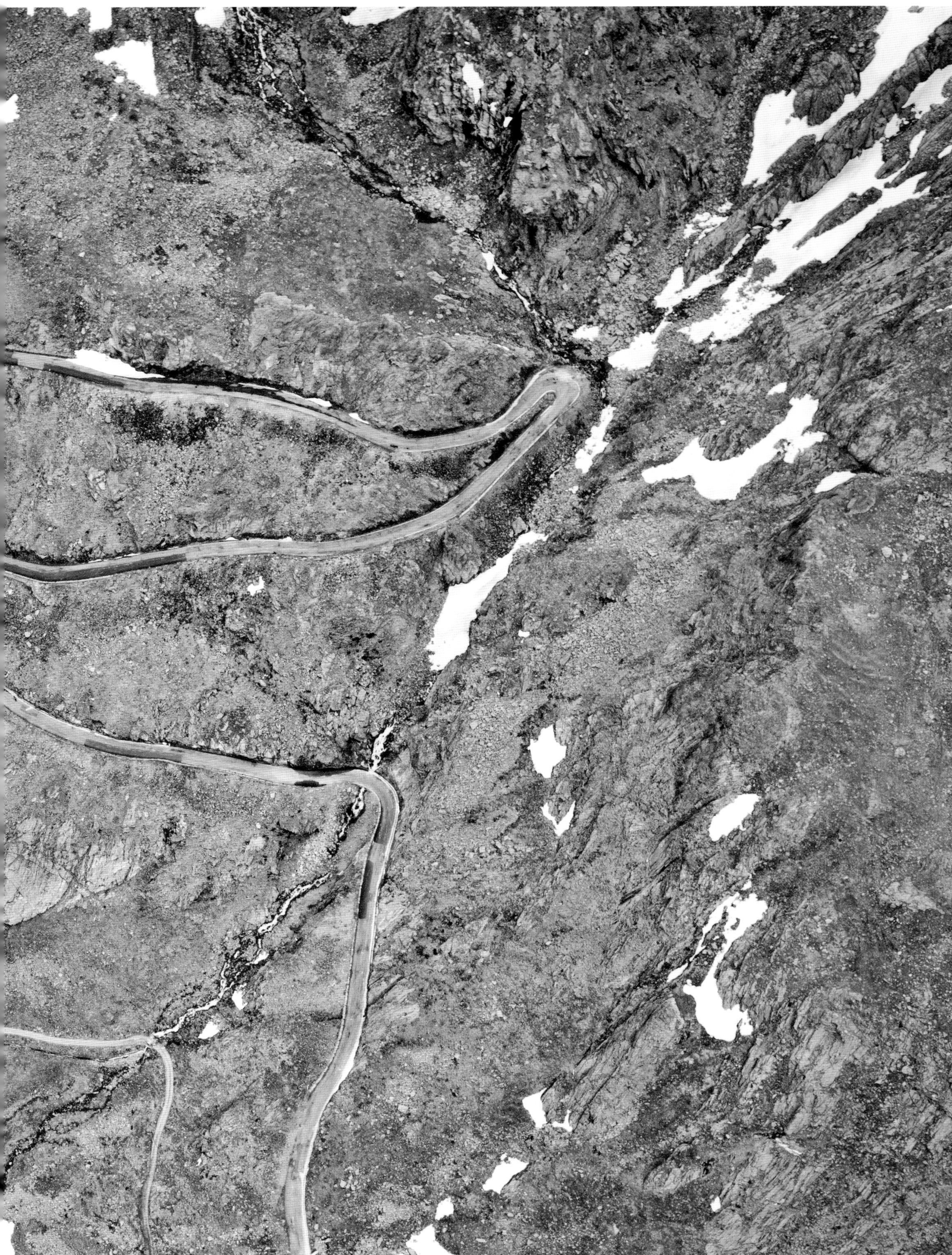

ROAD TO LIVIGNIO

an den Hängen empor, hat einen schwarzen Gürtel im Judo: wenig eigene Energie aufwenden, den Gegner angreifen lassen, seine Kraft im eigenen Interesse kanalisieren. Das selbstvergessene Aufbäumen der Berge zieht die Straße empor, beinahe scheint es, als hätten die mächtigen Berge dort oben überhaupt nicht bemerkt, was sich an ihren Sockeln weiter unten tut. Und ehe sie sich versehen, hat sich die Straße zum Foscagnopass bereits zwischen ihnen hindurchgedrückt, der Monte Forcellina kann ihr nur noch nachsehen und auch am Monte Rocca ist sie vorüber, ehe der richtig anwesend sein kann. Man muss natürlich Verständnis haben, so ein Berg denkt ganz langsam und in ein paar Jahrhunderten, da kann einem zwischen gerade noch Steinzeit und auf einmal Heute schon mal der Bau einer Straße entgehen.

Und mit uns können die Gipfel eh nicht wirklich sauer sein, denn wir sind jetzt schon ins Tal von Livigno davongefahren, bleiben aber auch hier nicht lang, sondern rollen nach Süden davon. Aus Italien hinaus, in die Schweiz. Zweiter Versuch sozusagen. Eine schmale Straße huscht von der Grenze nach Süden und landet unvermittelt in den weit geschwungenen Rampen des Bernina-Passes, der sich hier aus dem weiten Poschiavino-Tal nach oben schwingt. Nach dem stillen Tasten über schmale, schüttere Straßen fühlen wir uns nun beinahe etwas überrumpelt. Der Bernina hat gewaltigen Dampf, mit rasantem Schwung schiebt er nach oben, seine Kehren segeln nur so durchs Gebälk der Berge. Ganz selten sortiert er kurze, harte Richtungswechsel hintereinander, sein Lieblingsthema sind weite Kehren. Und dann endlich stürzt er sich mit Gebrüll über eine letzte Kuppe, zum Bernina-Hospiz am Lago Bianco hinunter, prescht gleich aber sofort weiter. Hinunter, hinunter, hart an der Welle des Bergs entlanggleitend. Ein kurzes Slalomwedeln durch die Montebello-Kurve baut Tempo ab, dann sind wir am Talboden angelangt. Der Schwung des Bergs reicht aber weiter, spült uns an Pontresina vorbei und dann in weitem Bogen nach Norden ins Tal des Inn hinein.

Der Fluss ist schmal, das Tal ist breit, aber das ändert sich: Hinter S-chanf muss sich der Inn bereits wieder zwischen Bergen

from their thrall. The road relentlessly does its own thing and bravely presses ahead. It uses smart tactics to climb its way up the slopes like the nimblest of ninjas, expending as little of its own energy as possible, letting its opponent take the active role and channeling its strengths to its own advantage. The unselfconscious upward thrust of the mountains seems to drag the road along with it, almost forgetting what is going on down below. The road to the Foscagno Pass has squeezed its way between the peaks before they even notice. You fly past Monte Forcellina and Monte Rocca is over before it has actually begun. Remember that mountains like this have a very different sense of time, so that it is quite easy for them to miss the fact that a road may have been built here in the few centuries between the Stone Age and the present day.

Anyway the peaks can't really be that angry with us, because they have already allowed us to drive away from them and into the valley of Livigno. We don't stay long here either, but instead head south out of Italy for Switzerland. A second coming, you might say. A narrow road scrambles from the border toward the south and suddenly we find ourselves on the curving flanks of the Bernina Pass, which sweeps up from the broad Poschiavino valley. Having spent some time quietly trundling along spindly narrow roads, we are now a little surprised by the dynamic vigor of the Bernina Pass as it pushes upwards with urgent momentum. Its hairpin bends navigate a sovereign course through the mountains. Very occasionally the route throws in a series of sharp changes of direction, but otherwise consists of long hairpin bends.

Then, with one final roar, we rush over one last hilltop, down to the Albergo Ospizio Bernina Hotel on the shores of Lago Bianco, before immediately pushing on downward, pressing hard against the side of the mountain as it slides onward. A short slalom section through the Montebello curve slows the pace as we reach the valley floor. However the momentum of the mountain is unstoppable, washing us past Pontresina and then in a wide arc to the north into the valley of the Inn. Although the river is narrow, the valley is wide, but not for long: just beyond S-chanf, the Inn has to force its way back

HOTEL

VILLA FLOR
VILLA FLOR, SOMVIH 19
7525 S-CHANF
WWW.VILLAFLOR.CH

HOTEL CASTELL
VIA CASTELL 300
7524 ZUOZ
WWW.HOTELCASTELL.CH

RESTAURANTS

RISTORANTE PEPPINO'S
OLYMPIASCHANZE
VIA SAN GIAN
7500 ST. MORITZ
WWW.PEPPINOS.CH

LA SCARPETTA
VIA VEGLIA 11
7500 ST. MORITZ
WWW.LA-SCARPETTA.CH

AT. ST. MORITZER
MOBILWOCHE
UG. 1930

St. Mor

hindurchdrängen, die ihn gewaltig in die Zange nehmen, aber der Fluss hat bereits so viel Energie aufgebaut, dass er sich mit einigen Ellbogen-Bodychecks kurzerhand hindurchrempelt. Jetzt hat der den Respekt der felsigen Genossen, sie werden ihm auf seinem weiteren Weg fürs Erste in Ruhe ziehen lassen. Eiskalt, aquamarinblau und rauschend jagt der Inn dahin und wir folgen ihm gern. Bis Zernez geht das so, dann noch eine Biegung weiter nach Susch und hier geht uns neben dem hartnäckig dahintraben-den Wasser die Puste aus. Grußlos ziehen wir nach Westen davon, hinaus aus dem Tal und in die Berge hinauf. Nach wenigen Kilometern sind wir im Reich der Steinriesen, wuchten uns über den Flüelapass bis hinüber nach Davos.

Einmal rund ums Massiv des Jakobshorn geht es, in weitem Bogen zurück nach Süden und dann in Richtung Albula. Kurz vorher hüpfen wir auf einem kleinen Sträßchen, dahinkurvend in Bergwiesen, ins südlich gelegene Tal des gleichnamigen Flusses Albula und machen uns dort auf den letzten, weiten Weg der heutigen Etappe. Über den Albula-Pass zurück ins Inntal, nach Süden, vorbei am Abzweig zum Berninapass.

Der Inn, dieser alte Bekannte vieler Alpen-Reisen hat den größten Teil seines weiten Wegs zur Donau bei Passau noch vor sich, ist an dieser Stelle so schmal, dass man es sich erlauben kann, ihn am Ende des Tals in eine Röhre zu sperren und seine Klamm für die Straße zu nutzen. Nicht lang geht die Fahrt so, während der Inn unter uns ins Tal strömt, aus dem wir kommen, dann öffnet sich die Tal-Enge und wir sind draußen. Nebenan stolpert der Fluss durch sein steiniges Bett und scheint nicht zu ahnen, dass ihm gleich eine Freiheitsberaubung blüht – und das, nachdem er gerade eine glückliche Kindheit mit vollkommen antiautoritärer Erziehung genießen durfte: sich herunterstürzen aus den Schneegipfeln des Oberengadins, dann gemütlich in kalten, grünen Bergseen abhängen. Zuerst im Silsersee, dann im Silvaplanersee, im Champfèrersee und schließlich direkt hier bei uns. Im Sankt-Moritzer-See. Für den Inn geht die Reise gleich so richtig los, für uns ist sie auf dieser Etappe zu Ende. In Sankt Moritz, Engadin, Graubünden. Aber vermutlich wissen Sie eh, wo das ist.

through rocky terrain. Although the mountains seem unwilling to let it pass, the river has already built up so much energy that it quickly elbows its way through with a couple of body checks. Having earned the respect of its craggy comrades, the Inn will be allowed to continue its path relatively undisturbed for a time at least. The ice-cold, aquamarine waters of the river babble to us as they rush past and we feel inclined to follow. And so it goes until we reach Zernez, then we take another bend to Susch and here we run out of steam, unable to keep up with the Inn's insistent flow. Without so much as a goodbye, we turn west, out of the valley and up into the mountains. After a few kilometers we find ourselves in a land of stone giants, teetering across the Flüela Pass and over to Davos. We complete a circuit of the massif of the Jakobshorn, then make a wide arc back to the south and on toward Albula. Just before we get there, we switch to a small road, cutting through mountain meadows into the southern valley of the river that gives the area its name, Albula. From there we set out on the last, long leg of today's stage: over the Albula Pass back into the Inn Valley to the south, past the turn for the Bernina Pass.

The River Inn, an old friend from many trips to the Alps, still has most of its long journey to the Danube near Passau ahead of it and is so narrow at this point that it can be canalized at the end of the valley, allowing the gorge to be used for the road. This arrangement doesn't last long, the Inn flowing below us into the valley we have just come from. The narrow valley opens up and we find ourselves in wide open terrain. Next to us, the river stumbles along its stony bed, seemingly unaware that it is about to be imprisoned beneath the road, having enjoyed a happy childhood with no authoritarian limits: rushing down from the snowy peaks of the Upper Engadin, before relaxing in the cold, green mountain lakes. First the Silsersee, then the Silvaplana and the Champfèrersee before arriving right here where we are:

Lake Saint Moritz.Although this is where the journey really starts for the River Inn, for us it marks the end of our first stage. We've reached Sankt Moritz, Engadin, Graubünden. But you probably know that already.

HOTELS

HOTEL SOLDANELLA
VIA SOMPLAZ 17
7500 ST. MORITZ
WWW.HOTEL-SOLDANELLA.CH

BEVER LODGE
VIA MAISTRA 32
7502 BEVER
WWW.BEVERLODGE.CH

MÜSTAIR ST. MORITZ

Am östlichen Ende der Schweiz ist die Grenze turbulent. Österreich und Italien sind hier geschichtlich betrachtet keine klar abgesteckten Nachbarn, sondern haben sich entlang von Gebirgsketten und Tälern, unter dem Gerangel alter europäischer Adelshäuser bis in die Neuzeit ineinander verbissen. Es braucht also nicht viele Kilometer, um nach einem Start in die Schweiz hinein über den Umbrail-Pass geradewegs wieder das Land zu verlassen: Auf zum Stelvio-Pass, dem Stilfser Joch in Italien. Ohne eine Stippvisite zu diesem geschichtsträchtigen Kurvenwunder unter den Alpen-Pässen kann man eine Reise durch die Schweiz nicht angehen. Dann geht es aber nach Westen, über Bormio und einen zweiten Abstecher zum Gaviapass landen wir wieder in der Schweiz, direkt am Fuß des wilden Bernina-Pass, zwischen Poschiavo und Samedan. Zwischen Engadin und Veltlin. Zwischen allem was in Richtung Po-Ebene und Mittelmeer fließt und dem Wassersystem der Donau, die es bis zum Schwarzen Meer schaffen wird. Der Bernina ist nach dem heftigen Hakeln von Stelvio und Gavia ein flüssig zu fahrender Alpenpass, er bringt uns weiter in die Schweiz hinein. Nach einem weiteren Schwung über den Flüelapass und Albula-Pass sind wir zurück im Tal des hier noch sehr jungen Inn und beenden die Etappe in Sankt Moritz.

—

The border at the eastern end of Switzerland has had a turbulent history. In the past, Austria and Italy have not been the easiest of neighbors here, staking out their territories along the mountain ranges and valleys according to the age-old claims of Europe's aristocratic families until modern times. As a result it doesn't take long before you find yourself leaving Switzerland again via the Umbrail Pass: the Stelvio Pass takes you into Italy. No trip through Switzerland would be complete without a flying visit to this historic miracle among the region's curving Alpine passes. Our route then takes us west, via Bormio and a second detour to the Gavia Pass, when we arrive back in Switzerland, right at the foot of the wild Bernina Pass, between Poschiavo and Sameda, the Engadin and Valtellina. All the geological formations seem to flow towards the Po Valley and the Mediterranean and the great waterway of the Danube, which wends its way to the Black Sea. After the zig-zagging Stelvio and Gavia Passes, the Bernina affords a relatively smooth ride as it takes us further into Switzerland. Another hefty swing over the Flüela Pass and Albula-Pass takes us back to the valley of the River Inn, which is in its infancy here, and we end the stage in Sankt Moritz.

320 KM • 6 STUNDEN // 198 MILES • 6 HOURS

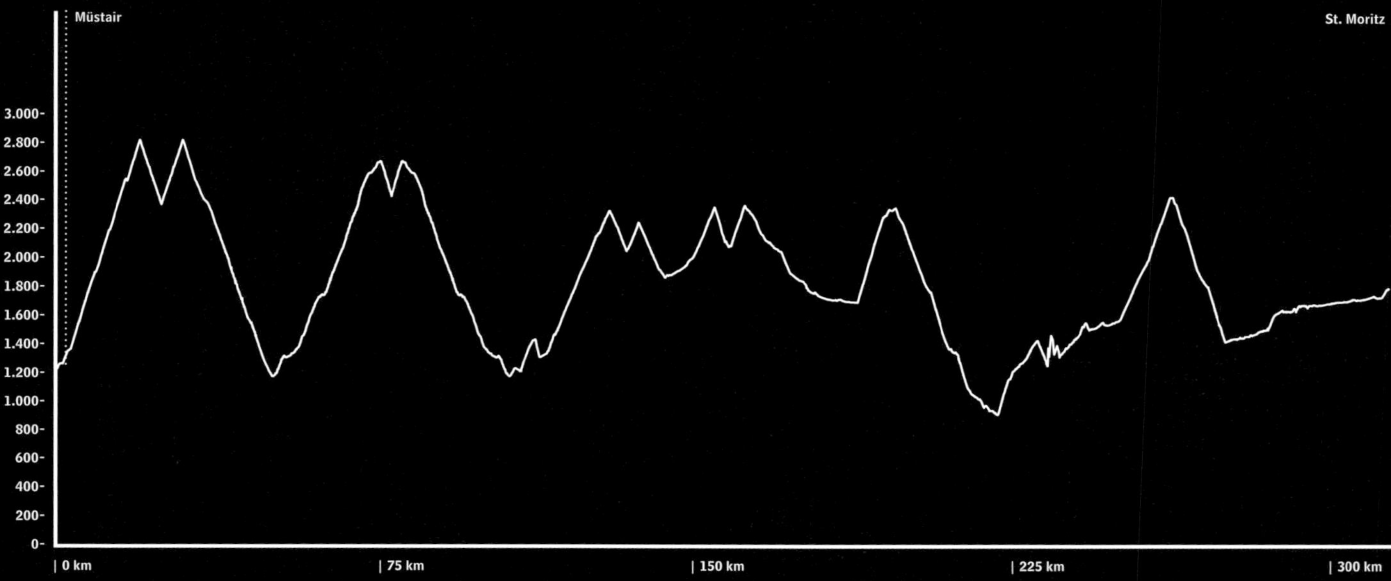

Davos
Klosters
Arosa
Weissfluh
Piz Buin
Silvretta Hochalpenstraße
Samnaun
Zollausschluss gebiet
Nauders
Scuol
Ardez
Lavin
Guarda
Susch
Zernez
Flüelapass
Schweizerischer Nationalpark
Pass dal Fuorn/ Ofenpass
Müstair
Santa Maria Val Müstair
Umbrailpass
Giogo d. S. Maria
Passo d. Stelvio
Stilfser Joch
Bormio
Livigno
Forcola di Livigno
Passo del Bernina
Piz Bernina
Pontresina
Samedan
St. Moritz
Julierpass
Malojapass
Albulapass
Zuoz
Poschiavo
Tirano
Sondrio
Aprica
Edolo
Ponte di Legno
Passo del Tonale
Mals
Glurns
Reschen
Valbondione
Foppolo
Morbegno
Parco Nazionale dello Stelvio
Adamello

SILSER SEE

ST. MORITZ GRIMSEL HOSPIZ

320 KM • 6 STUNDEN // 198 MILES • 6 HOURS

Sankt Moritz. Man weiß bei jedem Besuch der Königin des Engadins zuerst nicht so recht, ob nun ein Lustspiel folgen wird, ein Drama, eine Komödie, Passionsspiele, Thriller, Fire-and-Ice-Action oder doch nur eine leichte Operette. Irgendwie hat Sankt Moritz das ohnehin alles im Repertoire. Und deshalb einfach: Vorhang auf! – Grünes Wasser liegt spiegelglatt unter blauem Himmel.

—

Sankt Moritz. Every visit the Queen of the Engadin is a surprise. Should you expect a drama, comedy, romance, thriller, action adventure or just a frothy operetta? Somehow, Sankt Moritz seems to have it all in its repertoire. So… Curtain up! – An expanse of green water perfectly mirrors the blue sky.

MALOJAPASS

HOTEL

HOTEL ALTE HERBERGE WEISS KREUZ
OBERDORF 66
7435 SPLÜGEN
WWW.WEISS-KREUZ.CH

Scharfe Abrisskante am anderen Seeufer, der Übergang zum dichten Bergwald am Fuß des Piz Rosatsch ist wie mit der Linie gezogen. Das ganze Tal ist ein Bühnenbild: Im Nordosten der Ausgang des Inn, die Landzunge mit dem Waldhaus am See tritt daneben aus den Kulissen und bringt sich in Position. Am anderen Talende haben es sich Piz Julier und Piz Albana gemütlich gemacht, sie hängen im alpinen Plüsch Graubündens, lauern übers Geländer ihrer Loge und warten darauf, jeden Fehler auf der Bühne zu kommentieren. Es kommt keiner. Sankt Moritz ist für Profis, hier sitzt jeder Spruch, jeder Einsatz, jede Pointe. Die Stadt hat schließlich auch schon etwas Übung im internationalen Showbusiness. Der viereckige Turm des Badrutt's Palace mit seiner grünspanigen Kappe spielt eine Hauptrolle, ein paar Schritte dahinter ziert sich der spindeldürre Kirchturm von Sankt Moritz-Dorf zwischen unfrommen Luxus-Tempeln und scheint zu überlegen, ob der Teufel nun wirklich Prada oder doch Gucci trägt.

Wir wollen allerdings eine andere Vorstellung nicht verpassen und stürmen nach Süden aus der Stadt hinaus. Winken dem Grand Hotel des Bains zu, das ein wenig wie

You can make out a sharp edge on the other side of the lake, where the transition to the dense mountain forest at the foot of Piz Rosatsch looks like it has been drawn with a ruler. The whole valley is like a vast stage set: the River Inn makes its exit to the northeast, while the spit of land with the Waldhaus am See at the end emerges from the background to take up position like a leading lady. At the other end of the valley, Piz Julier and Piz Albana have found a comfortable place for themselves, enjoying the plush alpine surroundings of Graubünden, peering over the rails of their box and waiting to comment on every little mishap on the stage. Happily there are none. Professionalism is a byword in Sankt Moritz, so every syllable, every gesture and every entrance really counts.

After all, the city already has some experience with international show business. The square tower of Badrutt's Palace Hotel with its green copper roof is the leading lady in this particular drama. The spindly shape of the church spire in Sankt Moritz-Dorf is content to play second fiddle here, squeezed between the temples to worldly luxury and trying to decide whether the devil really does wear Prada, or is it Gucci? However, there's

SERIE DI GALLERIE

SAN BERNHARDINO PASS

die Deko einer überlebensgroßen Modelleisenbahn wirkt, und rollen dann durch Champfèr, vorbei an Silvaplana, dem Dorf am Fuß des Julierpasses. Hinter dem Ende des Silsersees schwingt sich die Straße in sahnigen Slalombögen weiter, links und rechts reihen sich die Häuser von Maloja. Und dann geht es bergab: Schussfahrt. Runter nach Chiavenna, wieder einmal hinaus aus der Schweiz. Das geht im rätoromanischen Süden des Landes ganz leicht. Der warme Teil Europas ist hier immer in Reichweite, man spürt mediterrane Schwingungen. Vom Comer See wehen warme Winde herauf, die ein wenig früher bereits in Mailand waren. Die ganze Gegend lässt mit markantem Zungenschlag gewaltig das R rollen. Wer das jetzt aber pauschal einer „italienischen" Sphäre zuschreibt, trifft mit Anlauf knapp daneben.

Auch wenn die südliche Schweiz immer schon unter dem Einfluss Italiens stand, beginnend in der Steinzeit, weiter über Bronzezeit und Antike, hinein ins Mittelalter und in die Neuzeit, muss man sich das wohl eher wie die Wellen einer europäischen Kultur-Dünung vorstellen. Ebbe und Flut der politischen Reiche und Einfluss-Sphären, die Alpen darin als natürliche Festung in dieser Brandung. Die aufsteigenden Römer sollen etruskische Völker in den Norden verdrängt haben, die sich dann in den schwer zugänglichen Alpentälern niederließen und dort sesshaft wurden. Das Imperium drängte nach, Handel, Militär und Zivilisation folgen – aus den Bewohnern der Alpen wurde im kulturellen Vollwaschgang der Jahrhunderte das, was wir heute als rätoromanische Kultur kennen. So zumindest geht eine Theorie, die erklären möchte, weshalb die Schweiz neben Deutsch, Französisch und Italienisch auch das komplexe, kernige Rätoromanische als vierte offizielle Amtssprache führt. In Chiavenna schwenken wir zurück nach Norden, 30 Kilometer später haben wir auf der Strada Statale 36 zur Splügenpass-Höhe wieder einmal die Grenze in die Schweiz erreicht. Durch weite Grasmatten hat sich die Straße zur Passhöhe emporgearbeitet und landet an ihrer höchsten Stelle bei über 2.100 Metern. Im Sommer ist die Flanke von Süden ein schwungvoll zu fahrendes Uptempo-Vergnügen, im Winter seit alters her eine Lawinenfalle. Die offenen Hänge des umgebenden Geländes wirken wie Rutschbahnen,

another performance we don't want to miss, so we soon make our way south out of the city. We wave as we pass the Grand Hotel des Bains, which looks a bit like something from a larger-than-life model railway, and then cruise through Champfèr, passing Silvaplana, the village at the foot of the Julier Pass. Beyond the far end of Lake Sils, the road follows a gentle slalom course, the houses of Maloja lining up on the left and right. We then take a plunge, descending to Chiavenna and crossing out of Switzerland once again.

It's a very smooth transition to the Romansh-speaking south of the country. Europe's warmer climes are never far away here and you can feel the Mediterranean vibe wherever you go. The warm winds blowing in from Lake Como are a reminder that Milan isn't so far away. The characteristic rolling R's are heard on every local tongue. However, don't make the mistake of associating this sound with an innate regional "italianità". Even though the influence of Italy has always been strong in southern Switzerland, starting in the Stone Age, continuing through the Bronze Age and classical antiquity, into the Middle Ages and modern times, you should imagine it more like waves of European culture. The Alps acted as a natural fortress against the rise and fall of political empires and spheres of influence. Enjoying ascendancy, the Romans are said to have displaced the Etruscans in the north, pushing them into the inaccessible Alpine valleys, where they eventually settled. As the territory of the Roman empire grew, trade, military activity and civilization followed, slowly transforming the culture of the inhabitants of the Alps into what we recognize today as Rhaeto-Romanic. At least that's one theory to explain why Switzerland also uses complex, robust Romansh as its fourth official language alongside German, French and Italian. In Chiavenna we turn back to the north and, 30 kilometers later, we find ourselves once again on the border with Switzerland on the Strada Statale 36 at the Splügen Pass. The road has worked its way up to the top of the pass through wide patches of grass and now reaches its highest point at over 2,100 meters above sea level. In summer the southern side is a pleasantly lively ride, but in winter it has always been an avalanche hazard. The open slopes of the surrounding area act like slides, funneling the masses of snow to the lowest

HOTELS

HOTEL SONNE
GOTTHARDSTRASSE 76
6490 ANDERMATT
WWW.HOTELSONNEANDERMATT.CH

BOUTIQUE HOTEL THE RIVER HOUSE
GOTTHARDSTRASSE 58
6490 ANDERMATT
WWW.THERIVERHOUSE.CH

RADISSON BLU HOTEL
BÄRENGASSE 1
6490 ANDERMATT

Trichter für die Schneemassen – an ihrem tiefsten Punkt verläuft die Straße. Alte Galerien erinnern daher an die Versuche, Säumer und Fuhrleute vor dem eiskalten Treiben der Natur zu schützen, und vielleicht auch daran, dass unser „Soulful Driving“ ein Privileg ist. Wir haben es der Natur und dieser Landschaft abgetrotzt. Sei demütig, sagt der Splügenpass von Süden her. Sei dankbar, sagt er im Norden. Hinter der Grenze stürzt sich die Passstraße nämlich wieder einmal in krachenden Kehren den Berg hinunter, links und rechts und links und rechts, bis du schwindelig und glücklich bist.

Unten in Splügen fließt der Hinterrhein daher, wir folgen seinem Tal nach Westen. Und jetzt heißt es: Aufpassen! Nur nicht aus Versehen in die Röhre des San-Bernardino-Tunnels fahren, denn die ist ein Schwarzes Loch. Saugt dich ein, pumpt Dich als sedierte Rohrpost unter den Bergen hindurch und spuckt dich auf der anderen Seite wieder heraus. Ein schreckliches, taubes Schicksal, das Menschen erleiden, die unterwegs sind, um von A nach B zu kommen. Nicht mehr. – Und deshalb: am Ende des flachen Talbodens auf die Straße zum San Bernardino zielen, dem Sirenengesang der gut ausgebauten Auffahrten zum Tunnel hin widerstehen, der schmalen Straße zum Himmel folgen. Nummer Dreizehn in Blau – gut. Dreizehn in Rot – böse. Eigentlich leicht zu merken. Und die Belohnung folgt augenblicklich: Sechzehn Serpentinen juchzen und jodeln gleich auf den ersten paar hundert Metern, dann räubert die Straße dem Berg entgegen. Schwingt und surft und drängt voran, dass es eine wahre Freude ist, und landet dann am alten „Hospiz St. Bernhard“, einem grauen, mürben Kasten am kleinen Laghetto Moesola, dieser Schmelzwasserlache in einer Mulde auf der Passhöhe. Graue Felsplatten drängen sich in feisten Schichten durch die Grashaut der Berge, ein paar Meter weit buckelt die Straße noch empor, dann stürzt sie ins Tal nach Süden hinunter. Dichter Nadelwald steigt die Hänge am Fuß auf dieser Seite empor, Serpentinen wirbeln im Dunkelgrün hinunter. Dann sind wir im Tal der Moesa angekommen, folgen ihm zwischen mächtigen, grünen Bergen nach Süden, für einen langen Traum. Hinaus aus dem Kanton Graubünden, hinein ins italienischsprachige Tessin. Bei Bellinzona fließt die Moesa in den Ticino, hier geht es

point on the pass, the road. Old rock galleries can be seen along the way, a reminder of previous attempts to protect drovers and carters from the icy ravages of nature, and perhaps also reminding us of how lucky we are to be taking this “soulful drive”. We negotiate the Splügen Pass in a mixture of humility and gratitude for what has been hewn from the natural landscape for our benefit. Once we cross the border, the pass road tumbles down the mountain in a series of crashing bends. We switch left, right, left, right, leaving us dizzy but happy.

The Hinterrhein flows onward down in Splügen and we follow the river valley to the west. A little care is needed here to avoid accidentally entering the black hole that is the San Bernardino tunnel. Otherwise you'll get sucked in, pumped under the mountains and spat out on the other side. This is the terrible, stifling fate suffered by people who simply need to get from A to B. Therefore: when you reach the end of the flat valley floor, take the road to San Bernardino, resisting the siren song of the well-built entrances to the tunnel and instead following the narrow sky road. It's really quite easy to remember: if the number thirteen is blue, then all is well, but if it is red, then you're on the wrong road. It's not long before you get your reward: there are sixteen sharp serpentines to cheer your way on the first few hundred meters, then the road tears into the mountain. We swing and sway as we press ahead, enjoying the ride, finally ending up at the old “Hospiz St. Bernhard” hostel, a gray, crumbling box on the shore of Laghetto Moesola, a tiny meltwater pool in a hollow at the top of the pass. Slabs of gray rock push their way through the grass-covered the mountains in thick layers and the road twists upward for a few meters, before it plunging down into the valley to the south. Dense coniferous forest rises up the slopes on this side, while hairpin bends spiral into the green depths below. We've arrived in the valley of the River Moesa, which we now follow southwards through mighty, green mountains as if in a dream. Leaving behind the canton of Graubünden, we enter Italian-speaking Ticino. The Moesa flows into the River Ticino in Bellinzona, which is where we start to head north again. The charms of the “Fiume Ticino” only accompany us as far as Biasca, after which the river swings westward, while we stay on a clear

RESTAURANT

BERGGASTHAUS SUSTENPASS HOSPIZ
SUSTENSTRASSE
6484 WASSEN
WWW.SUSTENPASS-HOSPIZ.CH

für uns wieder nach Norden. Den „Fiume Ticino“ haben wir aber nur bis Biasca als Reisegenossen, dort schwenkt er nach Westen, wir bleiben auf klarem Nordkurs. Am Ende des Tals wartet die Straße zum Lukmanierpass. Wir sind jetzt vollkommen jenseits jeden touristischen Interesses, mitten im Flow des Fahrens angelangt. Völlige Ruhe im Auge des Sturms, Fahren als Zen-Meditation. Surfen über den Lukmanier bis Disentis/Mustér. Dass wir hier wieder im rätoromanischen Graubünden angekommen sind, nehmen wir nur am Rande wahr. Neben uns stolpert schüchtern ein kleiner Bach den Berg hinunter, er kommt aus den Fels- und Schneefeldern am Ende dieses eisigen Gebirgstals, in ein paar Wochen wird er als mächtiger Rhein in die Nordsee fließen... Vielleicht werden wir ihn auf dieser Reise wiedersehen? – Auf zum Oberalppass, gekrönt von derben Felszinnen, hinein in den Kanton Uri und immer weiter hinunter nach Andermatt. Die Gebirgsstadt im Tal der Reuss ist eine letzte Verschnaufpause, ein Nadelöhr auf der weiteren Fahrt. Jetzt wird es dramatisch: Mahlende Felszähne greifen am Urnerloch im Norden Andermatts ineinander, wollen die Straße zu Staub zermahlen, dann geht es unaufhaltsam in die Schöllenen-Schlucht hinein. Die alte Teufelsbrücke dort wirkt wie die Reste einer Troll-Festung. Man sieht der wilden Führung in der Enge der Schlucht sofort an, wie entschlossen sie gebaut wurde, um Andermatt aus dem Talboden darunter zu erschließen.

Vorüberhuschendes Halbdunkel von Galerien, Tunnel, dann sind wir draußen – und nehmen natürlich auch noch den Abstecher in Göschenen zum Göscheneralpsee. Pause, dann wieder fahren, fahren, fahren. Auf zum Sustenpass. Der geht in Wassen los, ein paar Kilometer Fahrt in nördlich Richtung hinter Göschenen. Windet sich durch eine majestätische Bergwelt mit atemberaubenden Ausblicken ins Weite, in die umgebenden Täler hinein. Und dann sind wir in Innertkirchen, der Tag ist alt und ebenso müde wie wir. Einen letzten Pass müssen wir bis ans Ende der Tagesetappe noch fahren: Den Grimsel. Über gewaltige Treppenstufen hinweg zieht er sich den Berg hinauf, passiert Staumauern und -seen und am größten von ihnen, dem Grimselsee, biegen wir nach rechts über die Staumauer ab. Zum Grimsel Hospiz, dem dramatisch gelegenen Ziel dieser Fahrt.

north course. The road to the Lukmanier Pass awaits us at the end of the valley. We are now completely oblivious to any tourist interests, focused entirely on the drive. Like the absolute calm in the eye of the storm, driving becomes something like Zen meditation. As we surf over the Lukmanier Pass to Disentis/Mustér, we barely notice that we have arrived back in Graubünden. Next to us a little stream shyly tumbles down the mountain, emerging from the rock and snow fields at the end of this icy mountain valley. In a few weeks it will flow into the North Sea as the mighty Rhine... Who knows, maybe we'll see it again on this trip? – We press on to the Oberalp Pass, crowned by rugged rocky pinnacles, entering the canton of Uri and descending to Andermatt.

This mountain town in the Reuss valley offers a last respite, a chance to pause before the final part of the journey. This is where things start to get dramatic: grinding teeth of rock mesh at the Urnerloch Tunnel to the north of Andermatt, seemingly intent on turning the road to dust. We then continue without a break into the Schöllenen Gorge. The old Devil's Bridge there looks like the remains of a troll fortress. You can immediately see from the wildness of the route through the narrow gorge just now much determination it took to reach Andermatt from the valley floor below.

We pass through the semi-darkness of galleries and tunnels, and then we're out in the open again. Naturally we take the detour to the Göscheneralpsee in Göschenen, where we take a break. Then it's drive, drive, drive once again to the Susten Pass. This starts in Wassen, a few kilometers to the north beyond Göschenen. We find ourselves winding through a majestic mountain world with breathtaking views into the vastness of the surrounding valleys. By the time we reach Innertkirchen, the day is almost done, just like ourselves. There is one last pass we need to negotiate before we complete today's stage: the Grimsel. The road drags itself up the mountain over gigantic stepped slabs, passing dam walls and lakes. We turn right at the largest of these, the Grimselsee, crossing along the dam wall. Finally we reach the venerable Grimsel Hospice hotel, the dramatically situated final destination of today's trip.

HOTELS

GRIMSEL HOSPIZ
AM GRIMSELPASS
3864 GUTTANNEN
WWW.GRIMSELWELT.CH

HOTEL UND NATURRESORT HANDECK
GRIMSELSTRASSE
3864 GUTTANNEN
WWW.GRIMSELWELT.CH

GRIMSEL HOSPIZ
HOTEL · RESTAURANT

HOTEL
GRIMSEL HOSPIZ
RESTAURANT
BUS

ST. MORITZ GRIMSEL HOSPIZ

Wir starten im Engadin, fahren von Sankt Moritz in Richtung der italienischen Grenze. Mit dem Malojapass grooven wir uns ein, schnuppern danach über Chiavenna in Richtung Splügenpass fahrend ein wenig italienisch-mediterranes Flair. Ein paar Kilometer später sollte man auf dieser Etappe so richtig warmgefahren sein, denn jetzt geht es über den San Bernardino, einen der großen Pass-Hauptdarsteller der Schweizer Alpen. In einer mächtigen Königsetappe führt uns der Sankt Bernhard, wie er auf Deutsch genannt wird, nach Süden. Wir verlassen Graubünden, fahren bei Bellinzona ins italienischsprachige Tessin und haben hier beinahe wieder den Norden Italiens erreicht. Mailand ist von hier nur noch ein Katzensprung. Wir schwenken dann aber wieder nach Norden ab, schließen uns mit dem Lukmanierpass wieder das Innere der Schweiz auf und landen erneut im rätoromanischen Graubünden. Über den Oberalppass geht es in den Kanton Uri, bei Andermatt haben wir das dramatische Finale dieser Tagesetappe erreicht: durch die Schöllenen-Schlucht ins Tal der Reuss – dann über den Sustenpass bis Innertkirchen im Kanton Bern. Und nun haben wir das Ziel endgültig vor Augen: die Fahrt hinauf zu den Stauseen am Grimselpass.

–

We start out in Engadin, travelling from Sankt Moritz toward the Italian border. We find our groove on the Maloja Pass, taking time to explore a little and passing through Chiavenna in the direction of the Splügen Pass and enjoying a little Italian Mediterranean flair. A few kilometers later and we've really hit our stride on this stage, traversing the San Bernardino Pass. This is one of the major passes in the Swiss Alps and certainly provides a majestic setting as it sweeps us south. We leave Graubünden, entering Italian-speaking Ticino at Bellinzona and finding ourselves once again within reach of northern Italy. Milan is just a stone's throw away. But then we swing north again, joining up with the Lukmanier Pass to dive back into Switzerland's interior and land again in Romansch territory in Graubünden. Crossing the Oberalp Pass to the Canton of Uri, near Andermatt we come to the dramatic finale of this day's stage: we make our way through the Schöllenen Gorge into the Reuss Valley, then over the Susten Pass to Innertkirchen in the canton of Bern. Finally we have our destination in our sights: the climb to the man-made lakes on the Grimsel Pass.

320 KM • 6 STUNDEN // 198 MILES • 6 HOURS

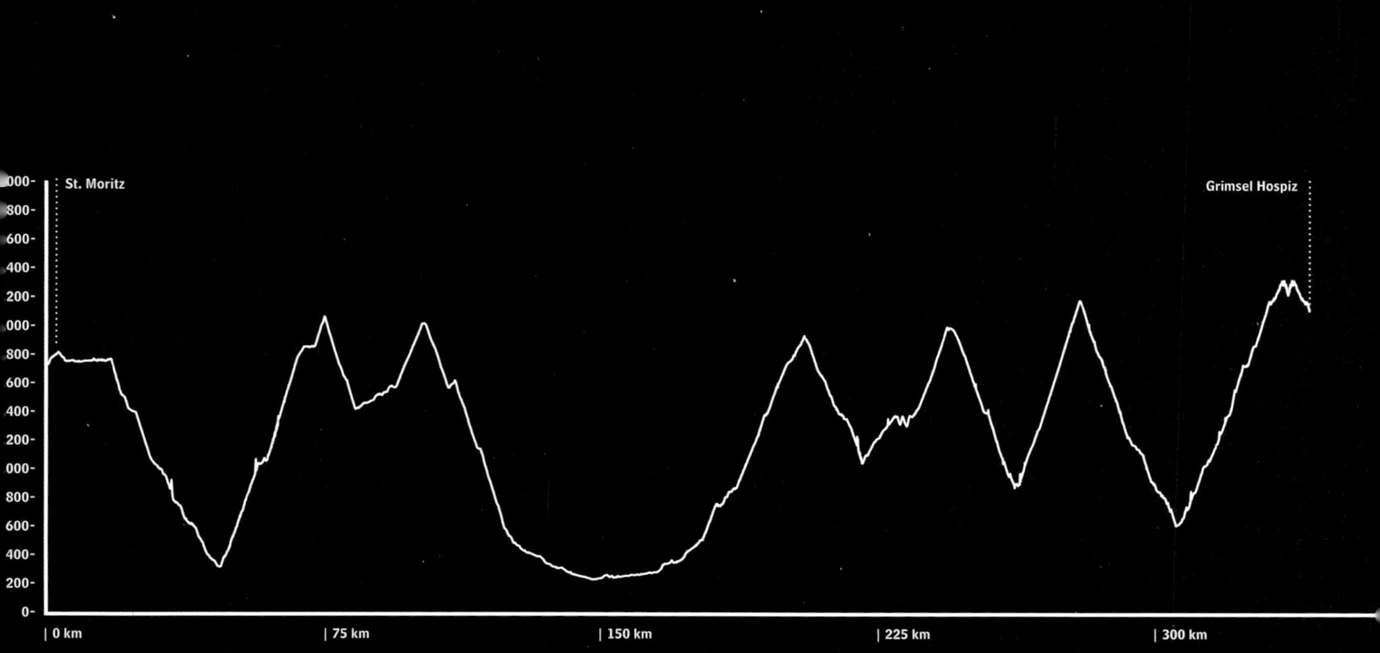

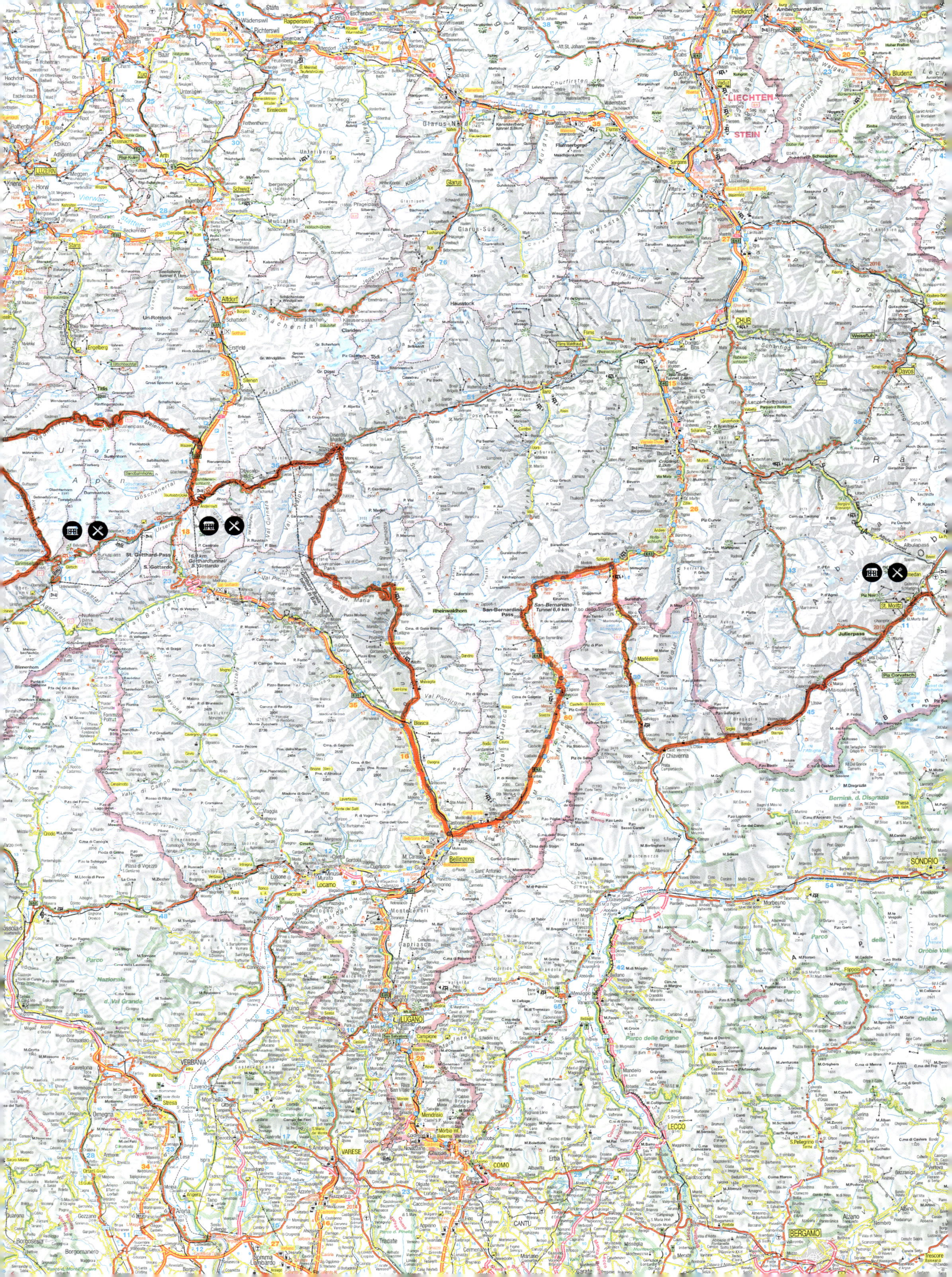

LUZERN
Zug
Schwyz
Altdorf
Glarus
Chur
Davos
Bludenz
Feldkirch
LIECHTENSTEIN
Sargans
St. Gotthard-Pass
Gotthardtunnel
San-Bernardino-Pass
San-Bernardino Tunnel 6,6 km
Rheinwaldhorn
Biasca
Bellinzona
Locarno
LUGANO
Chiavenna
Madesimo
St. Moritz
Julierpass
SONDRIO
Morbegno
VERBANIA
VARESE
COMO
LECCO
BERGAMO
CANTÙ
Mendrisio
Campione
Orbie
Parco delle Grigne

GRIMSELPASS

GRIMSEL HOSPIZ MARTIGNY

350 KM • 6 STUNDEN // 218 MILES • 6 HOURS

Eiskalt knistert der Morgen in den Bergen. Nebelfetzen treiben oben an der Höhe des Grimselpasses über den Totensee. Wir sind in den steinernen Eingeweiden der Alpen auch mental angekommen, fühlen eine geheimnisvolle Verbindung zu diesem harten, stoischen Ort. So schnell wollen wir nach der Nacht im Gebirge nicht wieder hinunter ins Tal, und deshalb bleiben wir in der Höhe.

—

It's a crisp, cold morning in the mountains. Wisps of fog drift over the waters of the Totensee at the height of the Grimsel Pass. In psychological terms we have pierced the stony heart of the Alps, feeling a mysterious connection to this hard, silently resilient place. After a night in the mountains, we're reluctant go back down to the valley too quickly, which is why we're staying up high.

FURKAPASS

HOTEL
GLETSCHER-RESTAURANT
BELVEDERE

HOTEL FURKABLICK

Wir fahren nach Westen, ungeachtet der tief hängenden Wolken, die in dunklen Rudeln um die Bergzinnen streifen und mit nassem Atem die Welt tränken. Weg von der Passhöhe, auf die Oberaar-Panoramastraße, die in den Geröllhalden und Felshängen oberhalb des Grimselsees entlang führt. Früher haben sich im Talboden unterhalb dieser Stelle Lauteraargletscher und Finsteraargletscher zum Aargletscher vereinigt, heute liegt nun noch der aufgestaute Grimselsee als riesige Lache von Schmelzwasser in der felsigen Rinne. Tief unter uns macht er sich breit, als kalkgraues Wassermonster liegt er im Gelände, während wir uns auf der Straße in der Flanke des Bergs immer weiter vorarbeiten. Allein dieses Fahren über den Wassermassen ist atemberaubend, die Panoramastraße hat aber noch eine letzte Pointe zu erzählen: Sie schwenkt langsam nach Südwesten, während der Grimselsee stetig Richtung Nordwest ausweicht – dann tut sich vor uns noch eine weitere Staumauer auf. In ungelenkem Bogen versperrt sie dem Wasser des Oberaar-Stausees den Weg ins Tal. Gespeist von einem weiteren Gletscher ist diese Welt karg und monochromatisch, felsgrau, eisblau, schneeweiß.

Dieser letzte menschengemachte Speicher füllt das äußerste Ende des Tals, weiter geht es hinter der Wasseroberfläche nicht mehr. Für uns ist hier am Parkplatz des Berghauses Oberaar deshalb Schluss, es geht zurück zur Grimselpass-Höhe, die uns nach dem Blick ins oberste Stockwerk der Alpen schon gar nicht mehr so martialisch vorkommt. Entspannt surfen wir die nach Süden schroff abfallende Grimselflanke über viele Serpentinen hinunter, dieses langsame, tastende Hinuntersteigen zum weiten Talboden fühlt sich an wie Abseilen aus der Wand: oben eine lebensfeindliche Welt, in die Menschen eigentlich nicht gehören, in der Eis und Geröll und Wolken das Sagen haben, unten die rettende Erdoberfläche in Grün. Es dauert eine ganze Zeit, bis wir den Boden erreicht haben, und hier, am Fuß des Grimselpasses treffen wir jetzt nach dem zur Donau strebenden Inn und dem noch jungen Rhein einen weiteren großen europäischen Fluss, der hier als Rinnsal seine ersten paar hundert Meter zurücklegt: die Rhône. Ihr Lauf beginnt am Ende eines

We head west, paying scant attention to the dark, low-hanging clouds that roam the mountain peaks in savage packs, soaking their surroundings with their wet breath. We draw away from the top of the pass, switching to the Oberaar scenic route, which passes along the scree slopes and rocky inclines above the Grimselsee. Eons ago, the Lauteraar and Finsteraar Glaciers merged to form the Aar Glacier in the valley floor below. These days a modern dam has turned the Grimselsee into a huge pool of meltwater encased in a bowl of natural rock. The lake lies far below us, spreading itself across the land like a chalk-gray aquatic monster, while we progress further and further along the side of the mountain. This drive above the mass of water is breath-taking enough, however the panoramic route has one last surprise up its sleeve: it slowly swings to the southwest, while the Grimselsee steadily pushes northwest – then another dam appears in front of us. Forming a clumsy arc, it blocks the path of the water from the Oberaar reservoir into the valley. Fed by another glacier, this is a barren and monochromatic world: slate gray, ice blue, snow white.

This last man-made lake fills the extreme end of the valley, bringing the road to a watery dead end. It's all over for us here at the parking lot of the Berghaus Oberaar hotel, so we return to the heights of the Grimsel Pass, which doesn't seem quite so impossibly impregnable to us now that we've seen life on the top floor of the Alps. In relaxed mood, we surf the side of the Grimsel Pass, as it slopes steeply to the south, following numerous serpentine bends. This slow, tentative descent to the wide valley floor feels like abseiling above a hostile world ruled by ice, scree and cloud, where people do not really belong.

Below us lies the welcoming green of the earth. It takes quite a while for us to reach the ground and here, at the foot of the Grimels Pass we encounter our third great European river. Having met the Inn on its way to the Danube and the Rhine in its relative infancy, we now come upon the Rhône, its first few hundred meters little more than a trickle. The river begins life

St. Gotthard
2091m
6860ft
A.C.S.

mächtigen Gletschers, der sich noch vor ein paar Jahrzehnten über einen deftigen Felsabsturz bis weit in dieses Tal heruntergeschoben hat, als gigantische Eiswalze. Aber heute ist der Rhône-Gletscher nicht mehr zu sehen. In wenigen, entschlossenen Zügen gewinnen wir nach ein paar Kilometern Fahrt am Talboden wieder Höhe und haben nun bald einen guten Blick auf die alte, vom Gletschereis blank geschliffene Felsrinne. Braun und grau und nackt zieht sie sich als enorme Narbe über einen Berghang. Der Gletscher selbst verbirgt sich jedoch im Inneren seines Jahrtausende alten Betts, ungefähr 50 Schritte muss man zu Fuß um eine Felsnase herum ins Tal gehen, um ihn zu sehen. 50 Schritte für 50 Jahre – so lang hat es gedauert, bis aus dem ehemals diese Welt dominierenden Eisriesen ein Schatten seiner alten Majestät wurde. Das Hotel Belvédère steht dort vorn in der Kehre, von seiner Terrasse konnte man einst das Cinemascope-Schauspiel des Eis-Stroms aus allererster Reihe verfolgen – jetzt ist die Aufführung zu Ende und auch die Lichter im Belvédère sind erloschen. Ein wenig traurig fahren wir weiter, über den Furkapass hinweg, bis nach Realp und haben dann in Hospental ein anderes Monument erreicht: die Auffahrt zum Gotthardpass.

Gestern sind wir nicht weit entfernt von hier in Andermatt nach Norden zum Susten und Oberalppass gefahren, jetzt geht es nach Süden. Druckvoll macht der Gotthard auf dieser Seite Streckenmeter und Höhenmeter. Obwohl der Großteil des transalpinen Verkehrs unter uns im Gotthardtunnel von Nord nach Süd zieht, ist die Passstraße hier oben immer noch gut befahren. Nebenan unternimmt die immer noch vorhandene alte Gotthardstraße eine Zeitreise, als schmales Kopfsteinpflasterband strebt sie den Berg hinauf. Am Gotthard-Hospiz treffen wir sie wieder und ab jetzt gehören wir ihr. Trippeln auf dem Kopfsteinpflaster die erste abfallende Rampe hinunter und stürzen uns dann in die Tremola: das 24-Kehren-Prachtstück alpiner Traditionsstraße, ein Klassiker der alpinen Grand-Tours, ein Manifest. Das hier ist der eigentliche Gotthard, die neue, aufwendig in den Fels gefräste Straße weiter im Westen nur ein Abklatsch, und wer den Tunnel nimmt, war ja nicht

at the end of a mighty glacier, which just a few decades ago pushed its way down into this valley across a massive rock-fall, as a gigantic roll of ice. These days, however, the Rhône glacier is nowhere to be seen. It takes us just a few determined moves to regain altitude after a few kilometers on the valley floor and soon we have a clear view of the old rock channel, polished by the glacial ice, an enormous brown-gray gash in the mountain slope. The glacier itself, however, is hidden inside its millennia-old bed. You have to walk around 50 paces around a rocky outcrop and down into the valley to see it. 50 steps for 50 years – that's how long it took for the ice giant that once dominated this world to become a shadow of its former majestic self.

The Hotel Belvédère lies up ahead on a bend. In the old days you could watch the cinemascope spectacle of the ice floe from the hotel terrace. Now, however, the performance is over and the lights in the Belvédère have also gone out. A little sadly, we continue across the Furka Pass to Realp, where we reach another monument in Hospental: the gateway to the Gotthard Pass. We weren't far from here yesterday in Andermatt when we drove north to the Susten and Oberalp Pass. But this time we're heading south. In terms of both distance and altitude, the figures associated with the Gotthard are certainly impressive. Although most of the transalpine traffic below us is moving from north to south in the Gotthard tunnel, it's still quite busy up here on the pass road. The old Gotthard route runs alongside, still seeming like a journey back in time, climbing up the mountain as a narrow cobblestone strip.

We come across it again at the Gotthard-Hospiz inn and from this point on our destinies join as one. We skitter down the cobblestones of the first sloping ramp and then plunge headlong into the Tremola: the 24 bends of this traditional alpine road make it a classic among alpine grand tours. This is the real Gotthard Pass. The new road, laboriously carved into the rock further west, is just a poor imitation. Anyone who takes the tunnel cannot even claim to have ever been in the mountains... The arrival down below in Airolo is always quite

HOTELS

ST. GOTTHARD HOSPIZ
PASSO DEL S. GOTTARDO 6780
6780 AIROLO
WWW.PASSOSANGOTTARDO.CH

GOTTHARDPASS

einmal in den Bergen... Unten in Airolo anzukommen ist immer sehr desillusionierend, nach all der Magie und Anderweltigkeit der zurückliegenden Kilometer vom Grimsel bis zum Gotthard trifft einen die Lebhaftigkeit und freundliche Alltagsbanalität der Zivilisation wie ein Schock. Etwas verloren treiben wir dahin und freuen uns deshalb ganz besonders über das erneute Treffen mit dem Ticino. An den haben wir gute Erinnerungen und deshalb nehmen wir seine Einladung zu einer Reise in seine Vergangenheit gerne an: durchs Val Bedretto zum Nufenenpass. – Vergessen Sie das intensive, beinahe gewalttätige Wesen der zurückliegenden Pässe, den jetzt wird alles leicht und galant. Ja, der Nufenen hat seine gelegentlichen wilden Momente, aber noch viel mehr gelassene: Bis auf 2.480 Meter steigt er an, und dass er damit zu den höchsten Passstraßen der Schweiz gehört, lässt er sich dabei nicht anmerken. Während andere Pässe auf jedem Meter das Gefühl von Schweiß und Plackerei verströmen, sich in steilem Gelände emporrackern, über mühselig ins Gestein gefräste Trassen, als Abenteurer und Hasardeure, macht der Nufenen größtenteils auf leichte Unterhaltung. Von majestätischen Panoramablicken in eine weite Gebirgs-

a let-down. After all the magic and otherworldliness of the stretch from the Grimsel Pass to the Gotthard Pass, the lively buzz and friendly routine banality of civilization come as quite a shock. Feeling a little lost, we find ourselves drifting and are therefore particularly happy to encounter Ticino again.

We have fond memories of this region, which is why we are happy to accept the invitation to journey into its past: through Val Bedretto to the Nufenen Pass. – Forget the intense, almost forceful nature of the previous passes. From now on, everything will be charming and easy-going. True, the Nufenen Pass has occasional wild moments, but even more serene ones: it climbs up to 2,480 meters without ever reminding you that it is one of the highest mountain passes in Switzerland. While you feel that other passes grunt and sweat on every meter, climbing up steep terrain via channels laboriously carved into the rock, like true adventurers and thrill-seekers, the Nufenen Pass is mostly about light entertainment. The road follows a lively course against the majestic backdrop of a vast mountain landscape,

ALETSCHGLETSCHER

MATTERHORN

MOOSALP

landschaft begleitet swingt er dahin. Als geschmeidiger Schenkelklopfer, sanft perlender Damenfreund. Und wenn du dann oben bist, eine leichte Schweißauflage spürst, ist dir klar: Der hat es in sich. Dieser Schlingel.

Gut gelaunt landen wir als ewige Freunde des Nufenen bei Ulrichen im Rhône-Tal. Die Rhône ist hier mit dem Temperament eines Teenagers unterwegs, sie hat es eilig, vermutlich wartet ein glutäugiges Date am Mittelmeer auf sie. Zielstrebig zieht sie mit Kurs Südwest durchs Land, viele Kilometer weit. Dörfer und kleine Städte begleiten sie, wir staunen nach den Stunden im Hochgebirge über Land und Leute. Bei Visp haben wir dann ein weiteres Ziel auf unserer Bucket-List: Ein Foto des Matterhorns muss sein. Ab nach Zermatt, denken wir, und wissen da noch nicht, dass ab Täsch kein Straßenverkehr mehr ins Tal darf. Nur per Bahn ist der Blick auf den Zacken des Matterhorns möglich – machen wir, klar. Und mit diesem großzügigen Abstecher haben wir auch ein Rezept entdeckt, wie der lange, gerade Weg mit der Rhône nach Südwesten doch seine Reize haben kann: einfach immer wieder in die fantastischen Seitentäler abbiegen. Mit der Straße nach Leukerbad machen wir den Anfang: luftiges Segeln entlang rhythmischer Straßenbögen, während bewaldete Berghänge links und rechts herunterrollen und dann am Ende des Tals vor den garstigen Fels-Riffen von Rinderhorn und Daubenhorn stranden. Kehrtwende, zurück ins Tal. Herrlich. Mal sehen, was als Nächstes kommt. Es ist kein Berg, es ist kein Tal, es ist kein Fluss: Es ist der Wechsel in die französischsprachige Schweiz. Ungefähr bei Sitten diffundieren die Sprachräume so langsam ineinander hinein, während die Stadt zu Beginn der 1900er-Jahre noch mehrheitlich deutschsprachig war, ist sie heute auf Französisch umgeschwenkt – und nennt sich Sion. Genau hier biegen wir in ein von Norden herandriftendes Tal ab, fahren viele Kilometer weit über eine schmale Straße bis zum Sanetschpass und darüber hinaus. Ruhe spüren. Bevor es zurück in Sion wieder zusammen mit der Rhône weitergeht. Nicht mehr weit. Keine 30 Kilometer mehr, dann haben wir in Martigny das Ende der Etappe erreicht.

a smooth, brawny crowd-pleaser. When you reach the top and feel yourself in a slight sweat, you know that this pass road is not without its challenges. We are in buoyant mood when, as firm fans of the Nufenen Pass, we arrive in Ulrichen in the Rhône Valley. The Rhône is like an excited teenager at this point. She's a girl in a hurry, and a bright-eyed date is probably waiting for her on the shores of the Mediterranean. Determined on her south-westerly direction, she travels many kilometers across the country. Several villages and small towns accompany her along the way and we marvel at the country and its people after spending so much time in the high mountains.

At Visp we have something else to cross off our bucket list: a photo of the Matterhorn is a must. Time to hit Zermatt, we think, as yet unaware that cars are no longer permitted to enter the valley from Täsch. You can now only view the peaks of the Matterhorn by train – which of course is not a problem. The lengthy detour enabled us to discover a way for the long, straight route with the Rhône to the south-west to reveal its charms: you just keep turning into the fantastic side valleys. We start with the road to Leukerbad: a smooth cruise along rhythmically winding bends, while wooded mountain slopes sweep down on the left and right.

We come to a stop at the end of the valley in front of the threatening crags of the Rinderhorn and Daubenhorn. We make a U-turn and head back up the valley. Fantastic. Let's see, what comes next. Before we know it, we cross the linguistic boundaries to find ourselves in French-speaking Switzerland. Around Sion, language slowly becomes more mutable. The city was still predominantly German-speaking at the beginning of the 1900s and was therefore known as Sitten, but has switched to the French name Sion in the intervening years. Here we turn into a valley that drifts from the north, drive many kilometers along a narrow road as far as the Sanetsch Pass and beyond. There's a distinct feeling of calm in the air. Then we return to Sion and continue along the Rhône. It's not far now. After less than 30 kilometers, we reach the end of the stage in Martigny.

HOTELS

HOTEL GORNERGRAT KULM
GORNERGRAT 3100 M
3920 ZERMATT VALAIS
WWW.GORNERGRAT-KULM.CH

LA GRANDE MAISON DE CHANDOLIN
RTE DU SANETSCH 13
1965 CHANDOLIN-PRÈS-SAVIÈSE
WWW.LAGRANDEMAISON.CH

ꞬRIMSEL HOSPIZ MARTIGNY

Vir starten am 2.164 Meter hohen Grimselpass. Bevor wir aber nach Süden ins Tal der Rhône hineinrollen, egen wir einen landschaftlich sehr eindringlichen Abstecher zum Oberaargletscher ein. Die am Berghaus beraar endende Panoramastraße darf bei einer Grimsel-Überquerung eigentlich nicht fehlen. Bis hierher st die Fahrt eindeutig schon atmosphärisch ungeheuer dicht, am Fuß des Grimselpasses angekommen, haben vir uns aber eine wahre Königsetappe erschlossen: Vorbei am Rhônegletscher nehmen wir den 2.429 Meter ohen Furkapass und sind nun direkt am legendären Gotthardpass (2.107 Meter) angelangt. Vor allem dessen üdflanke kann von leidenschaftlichen Kurven-Surfern unmöglich auf der neuen Asphalttrasse absolviert verden, eine Abfahrt nach Airolo über die traditionsreiche Kopfsteinpflaster-Route, der so genannten „Tremola“, ehört beinahe zum Pflichtprogramm einer Alpenüberquerung. Mit dem 2.439 Meter hohen Nufenenpass elangen wir ins oberste Stockwerk der Alpen, haben dann aber auch endgültig das Tor zu den Westalpen aufestoßen. Abstecher nach Täsch – hier startet die Bahn ins autofrei Zermatt und damit zum Matterhorn –, ach Leukerbad oder zum Sanetschpass bei Sion gehören zum weiteren Verlauf dieser bemerkenswerten Alpentappe, die in Martigny endet.

-

Ve start out on the 2,164-meter high Grimsel Pass. But before we head south into the Rhône valley, we first ake an impressive scenic detour to the Oberaar Glacier. The panoramic route that ends at the Berghaus Oberar hostel should not be missed when crossing the Grimsel Pass. Until now, the atmosphere on the journey as been extremely intense, but now, having arrived at the foot of the Grimsel Pass, we have entered a truly egal stage. Passing the Rhône Glacier, we take to the Furka Pass at 2,429 meters above sea level and find ourelves directly at the legendary Gotthard Pass (2,107 meters). Really passionate curve surfers will baulk at the lea of completing the southern side on the new asphalt route: a descent to Airolo via the traditional cobblecone route, the so-called “Tremola”, is almost obligatory when crossing the Alps. At 2,439 meters above sea evel, the Nufenen Pass takes us to the top of the Alps, finally opening the way to the Western Alps. A detour to äsch where the train to car-free Zermatt and the Matterhorn departs, to Leukerbad or the Sanetsch Pass near ion are part and parcel of this remarkable alpine stage, which ends in Martigny.

350 KM • 6 STUNDEN // 218 MILES • 6 HOURS

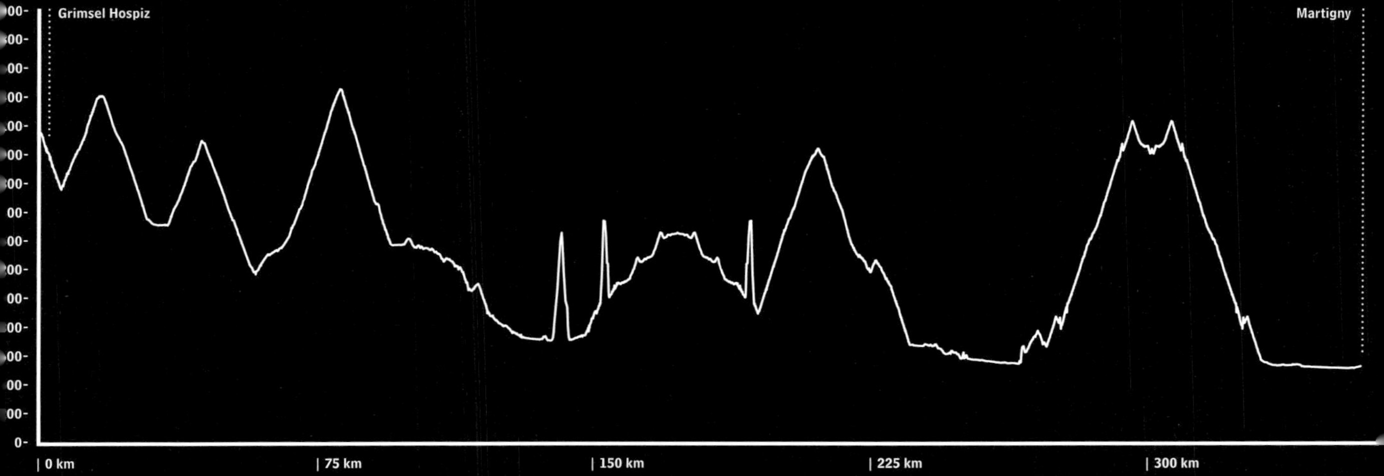

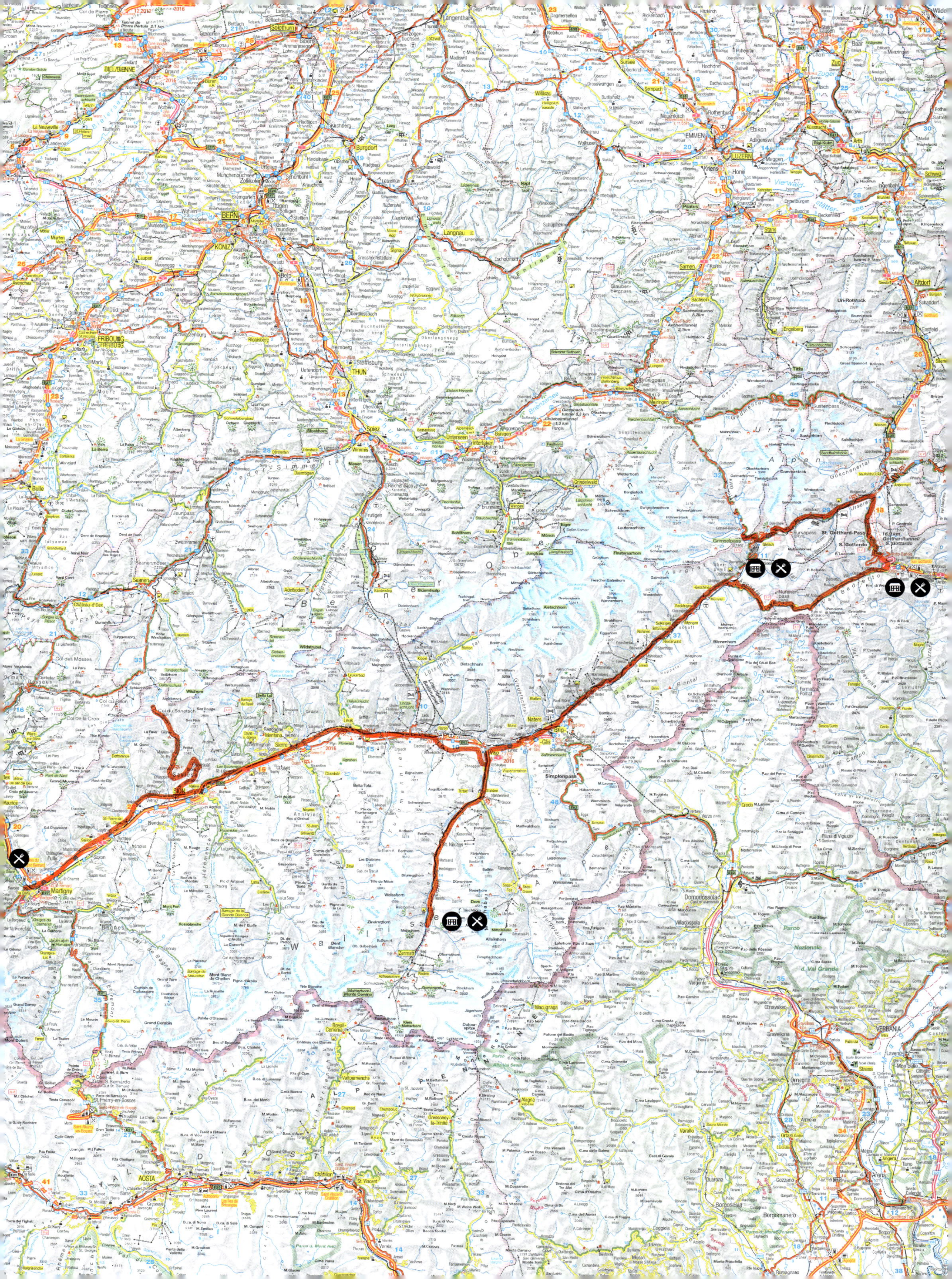

Solothurn
BIEL/BIENNE
Burgdorf
Langnau
EMMEN
LUZERN
BERN
KÖNIZ
FRIBOURG
THUN
Spiez
Interlaken
Grindelwald
Sarnen
Altdorf
Andermatt
St. Gotthard-Pass
Grimselpass
Sustenpass
Furkapass
Brig
Naters
Visp
Sierre
Sion
Martigny
Simplonpass
Zermatt
Domodossola
VERBANIA
Stresa
Aosta
Cervinia
Châtillon
Gressoney
Courmayeur
Bulle
Gstaad
Adelboden
Leukerbad
Lötschberg
Monte Rosa

GROSSER SANKT BERNHARD

MARTIGNY
LUZERN

510 KM • 10 STUNDEN // 316 MILES • 10 HOURS

Manchmal drängt ein lauwarmer Wind das Rhône-Tal herauf nach Martigny. Der nicht weit entfernte Genfer See macht sich bemerkbar und beinahe könnte man meinen, dahinter auch noch das Land jenseits der Alpen zu spüren: Lyon, Valence, Montélimar – und eine Ahnung der Provence.

—

Sometimes a warm breeze pushes its way up the Rhône valley as far as Martigny. You are reminded that Lake Geneva isn't far away and start to imagine you can almost feel the land beyond the Alps: Lyon, Valence, Montélimar – and a hint of Provence.

GROSSER SANKT BERNHARD

Aber vielleicht ist das alles auch nur schiere Einbildung. Wenn du aus den Bergen herunterkommst und die Sonne ins Tal scheint. Wenn die Weinberge an den Südhängen über der Stadt glitzern und am Mittag beinahe etwas Schwüle im Tal hängt. Wenn bläulicher Dunst das Gebirge im nun schon wieder fernen Osten verhüllt. Von dort oben kommen wir, die letzte Etappe mit ihren Riesen-Pässen steckt uns noch in den Knochen. Und jetzt sind wir beinahe schon am südlichsten Punkt unserer Tour angekommen – mit einem letzten Abstecher an den äußersten Zipfel des Südwestens der Schweiz runden wir auf der vor uns stehenden Etappe die Sache ab.

Das mag nach banaler Chronistenpflicht klingen, ist aber weit davon entfernt: Hier unten locken die weißen Bergriesen am Dreiländereck zwischen Frankreich, Italien und der Schweiz, große Namen des Alpinismus. Und deshalb geht es hinter Martigny erst einmal in einen Winkel des Rhône-Tals hinein, das Val d'Entremont. Gleich bei Martigny-Combe macht sich die Straße auf den Weg zum ersten Pass des Tages: Über dem Flusslauf der Dranse hangelt sie sich bis Valettes, dann zickzackt sie zum knapp 1.500 Meter hohen Col de Champex hinauf. Eine schmale Straße rauscht unbekümmert dahin, niedrige Steinmauern, Obstbäume und Schafgarben in den Wiesen begleiten sie. Es dauert gerade einmal die ersten paar Kilometern bis zur Gorges du Durnand, dann hast du den Flow dieser Straße verstanden: Elegant und flüssig ist dieser Pass, Motorradfahrer reiten ihn mit lässigem Schwung aus der Hüfte und im Auto steht das Lenkrad keine Sekunde lang still. Ständiges, präzises Nachziehen ist angesagt, auf und zu, laufen lassen, auf den Punkt fahren, bis es vor Begeisterung zwischen den Ohren kitzelt und du nur noch ununterbrochen jubeln magst. Dunkelgrüner Wald steigt mit uns die Berge hinauf, aber er bleibt der Straße fern, lässt ihr Luft und Licht.

Auf der anderen Seite entdeckst du dann: Das war jetzt erst die Phase zum Warmfahren. Hinter dem See von Champex stürzen sich Serpentinen ins Tal von Orsières hinunter und dann geht es weiter nach Süden. Ganz ernsthaft jetzt, denn der Blick auf die schneeweißen Zacken der Dents du Midi

But maybe it's just our minds playing tricks as we come down from the mountains to find the sun shining in the valley and the vineyards glistening on the southern slopes above the city. It feels almost sultry in the valley at noon. A veil of bluish haze descends on the mountains far to the east, where we've just come from. We can still feel the last stage with its giant passes in our bones. We have almost reached the southernmost point of our tour and round things off with a last detour to the extreme tip of southwest Switzerland.

This might sound like a chronicler's desire for completeness, but far from it: down here, the white mountain giants, big names in the mountaineers' roll of honor, beckon to us in this border region between France, Italy and Switzerland. That's why, after Martigny, you first enter a corner of the Rhône valley, the Val d'Entremont. At Martigny-Combe, the road rises to the first pass of the day, following the course of the Dranse to Valettes, then zigzagging up to the almost 1,500-meter high Col de Champex. A narrow road bowls along without a care in the world, bounded by low stone walls, with fruit trees and plentiful yarrow in the meadows beyond. After the first few kilometers to the Gorges du Durnand you start to understand the flow of the road: this pass is elegant and fluid. Motorcyclists negotiate its bends with a casual swing of the hip, while drivers find themselves constantly moving the steering wheel back and forth under their hands. You find yourself constantly correcting course, accelerating and slowing, letting the engine rip as you drive from point-to-point. The journey coaxes a sense of exhilaration from you until you just want to cheer continuously. Dark green forests climb the mountains with us, keeping their distance from the road, so the atmosphere is light and airy.

Once you reach the other side, you realize this was just the warm-up phase. Beyond Lake Champex, serpentines plunge down into the Orsières valley and then continue southwards. Things start to get serious now, because the view of the snow-white peaks of the Dents du Midi leave you in no doubt of the alpine ambitions of the next stage. The road leads straight to the Great St. Bernard

MUSEUM

HR GIGER MUSEUM
RUE DU CHÂTEAU 2
CHÂTEAU ST-GERMAIN
1663 GRUYÈRES
WWW.HRGIGERMUSEUM.COM

lässt keinen Zweifel an den hochalpinen Absichten der weiteren Etappe. Geradewegs zum Großen Sankt Bernhard führt die Straße, einem 2.500-Meter-Passungetüm hoch oben unter schroffen Zinnen, bedeckt mit Eis. Bis zum kleinen See an der Grenze nach Italien fahren wir, immer noch treiben Schneereste im Wasser, obwohl eine intensive Sonne auf den Pass-Sattel scheint. Ein beinahe schmerzhafter Sog zieht uns hinüber nach Süden, ins Aostatal und von dort vielleicht weiter, nach Turin und durch das Piemont, bis ans Mittelmeer. Wir könnten dort in der Sonne am Meer entlang fahren, hinüber in die Provence und über die Seealpen ... Aber dieser verträumte Moment dauert nicht lang. Heute fahren wir zurück nach Norden. Vielleicht kommen wir an einem anderen Tag wieder, für den Weg nach Süden.

Vierzig Kilometer später sind wir zurück in Martigny, hechten durch die Stadt und ins Rhône-Tal hinein. Bei Bex retten wir uns vor dem Schnellstraßen-Langeweile-Tod in Richtung Les Diablerets. Sanft und freundlich zuckelt ein kleines Asphaltband in weichen, grünen Wiesen dahin, wir blinzeln in die Sonne und schnuppern Bergluft. Zugegeben: Unten im Tal der Rhône wären wir längst am Genfer See und noch weiter, aber wir wollen ja nicht von A nach B, sondern fahren. Soulful Driving. Kurven und Landschaft, alles sehen. Bei Aigle sind wir beinahe schon wieder den Schnellstraßen der Westschweiz in ihr Netz gegangen, über das inmitten von Weinbergen gelegene Yvorne und Corbeyrier retten wir uns in Richtung des Lac de Hohengrin und rollen unermüdlich weiter in die Bergwelt hinein. Erst im kleinen Weiler L'Etivaz drehen wir vom Kurs nach Osten bei und wandern mit dem Gewirr der Täler und Hügel dieser verzauberten, sanften Landschaft nach Nordwesten. Wiesen duften, Kühe staunen, kleine Straßen stolpern selbstvergessen durch kleine Gehöfte und ringsum sitzen feiste Berge mit runden Schädeln auf breiten Sockeln. Der Lac du Vernex hat es auf das kleine Flüsschen Saane abgesehen und staut sie zu einem milchig-grünen Flecken, danach darf sie um ein paar Kilowatt Strom erleichtert wieder etwas zerzaust mit uns zusammen nach Norden, über die Grenze des Kanton Waadt in den Kanton Fribourg ziehen. Aber auch die Leute aus Fribourg haben kein Mitleid mit der Saane, kurz vor Albeuve blüht ihr ein Schicksal als Stausee-Futter ein zweites Mal – beleidigt raunt sie uns zu, sich das nicht noch einmal gefallen

Pass, which plows its way beneath craggy ice-covered mountain walls at 2,500 meters above sea level. We drive as far as the little lake that forms the border with Italy. Remnants of snow are still drifting in the water, although the sunshine on the saddle of the pass is intense. We feel ourselves drawn southward with an almost painful insistence into the Aosta Valley and from there perhaps further, to Turin, through Piedmont and on to the Mediterranean. We could then drive along the sun-kissed coast, crossing into Provence and then traversing the Maritime Alps... But it doesn't take long before this dream is abandoned. Today we're driving back north. Maybe we'll come back another day and head south.

Forty kilometers later we are back in Martigny, cutting through the city and on into the Rhône Valley. At Bex, we rescue ourselves from the deathly boredom of the expressway by heading in the direction of Les Diablerets. A narrow strip of asphalt takes us on a gentle trip through soft, green meadows. We find ourselves blinking in the sun and inhaling the bracing mountain air. Admittedly we would have reached Lake Geneva long ago if we had remained down below in the Rhône valley, but this trip isn't about getting from A to B. It's all about the drive. Soulful driving in curving landscapes, missing nothing. At Aigle we almost become entangled in the network of the expressways of western Switzerland once again, but make our escape via the vineyard-surrounded villages of Yvorne and Corbeyrier. We head in the direction of the Lac de Hohengrin and cruise onward into the mountains. Only at the small hamlet of L'Etivaz do we turn eastwards and head through the tangle of valleys and hills of this enchanted, gentle landscape, journeying northwest. We savor the sweet smell of the meadows. Cows turn their heads in surprise. Narrow byways blithely thread their way through small farmsteads. We find ourselves surrounded by plump, broad-faced, wide-bottomed mountains. The Lac du Vernex has decided to make the most of the little river Saane, damming it into a patch of milky-green green water. This is harnessed by a hydroelectric dam to generate a few kilowatts of electricity, before being allowed to head north with us, across the border of the canton of Vaud into the canton of Fribourg. However, the people of Fribourg take little pity on the Saane either and shortly before Albeuve it is used a second time to feed a reservoir. Clearly offended, the river whispers to us that it

60

ROUTE DE L'HONGRIN

zu lassen. Wenn die wüsste ... Zumindest bis Broc ist der Fluss noch ungebunden, wir haben zwar so ein Gefühl dass das nicht allzu lang so bleiben wird, wünschen der Saane aber alles Gute und überlassen sie ihrem weiteren Schicksal – uns zieht es nach Osten, über den Jaunpass ins Simmental hinein. Vorher haben wir aber noch ein Date mit Aliens: Am Ende der mittelalterlichen Stadt von Gruyères steht gedrungen und wachsam das Château de Gruyères, in einem der vorgelagerten Gebäude hat sich das HR Giger Museum samt Bar eingenistet. Bösartige Kreaturen aus Alpträumen lungern hier herum, mit offenen Brustkörben, toten Insektenaugen und klaffenden Reißzähnen in mächtigen Schädeln. Den Appetit auf ein echtes Greyerzer Fondue verdirbt einem das trotzdem nicht und deshalb verlassen wir Gruyère mit einem dramatisch duftenden Fresspaket, das im Gepäck freilich hermetisch abgedichtet untergebracht werden will. Bis zum Jaunpass haben wir uns allerdings zumindest den kernigen Duft des Greyerzer Käse aus den Klamotten wehen lassen, jetzt segeln wir schwungvoll hinein in den Kanton Bern, aus dem französischen Sprachraum der Schweiz in die deutschsprachige Schweiz. Das Tempo der Fahrt steigt, wir schneiden durch das weite Simmental, eine Landschaft voller Kultur und Geschichte, geradewegs auf die großen Seen der inneren Schweiz zu und landen endlich bei Spiez am Thunersee.

Dies ist das romantische Herz der Schweiz, eine Gegend, in der sich brachiale Berge und majestätische Seen zu einer Landschaft voll Schönheit und Ingrimm vereinen: An den Ufern von Thuner-, Brienzer-, Lungerner- und Sarnersee schwingt beinahe mediterraner Lebensstil mit, hier blinzelt die Welt durch dunkel getönte Sonnenbrillen in ein leichtes, entspanntes Lebensgefühl, während in direkter Nachbarschaft die Felsmonster von Eiger, Mönch und Jungfrau mit steinernen Zähnen mahlen, vor Eis schnauben, schneebedeckte Gipfel in zähen Wolkenkronen verbergen. Die Fahrt von Spiez entlang des Thunersees nach Interlaken gleicht einer eleganten Yacht-Fahrt, beinahe hörst du grünes Wasser an den glänzenden Holzrumpf klatschen, obwohl du auf der Straße unterwegs bist. Interlaken hat sich auf einer alten Schwemm-

won't put up with this indignity again. If it only knew... The river is allowed to run free at least as far as Broc. We get the feeling that it won't stay that way for too long, but we wish the Saane well and leave it to its fate, as we are drawn to the east. We cross the Jaun Pass into the Simmental Valley. But first we have a date with aliens: Château de Gruyères stands squat and watchful at the end of the medieval town of Gruyères. This is where the HR Giger Museum and bar have established themselves in one of the front buildings. Malignant creatures that are the stuff of nightmares lurk here, with open chest cavities, dead insect eyes and gaping fangs in mighty skulls. Hopefully this won't have spoiled your appetite for a real Gruyère fondue, which is why we leave Gruyère with a dramatically pungent food package, which of course needs to be hermetically sealed in the luggage compartment. By the time we've reached the Jaun Pass, however, we've got the tangy scent of Gruyère cheese out of our clothes and find ourselves sailing into the canton of Bern, leaving the French-speaking area of Switzerland to enter German-speaking territory. We increase our speed, cutting through the wide Simmental Valley, a landscape full of culture and history, heading straight to the great lakes in Switzerland's interior and finally ending up in Spiez on Lake Thun.

This is the romantic heartland of Switzerland, an area in which brutish mountains and majestic lakes come together to create a landscape full of beauty and simmering temperament: the lifestyle on the shores of Lake Thun, Lake Brienz, Lake Lungerner and Lake Sarnen is almost Mediterranean. Here the world is viewed through dark-tinted sunglasses, a sign of a light-hearted, relaxed attitude to life, despite the immediate vicinity of the rock monsters of the Eiger, Mönch and Jungfrau, grinding their stone teeth, snorting with icy breath, hiding snow-covered peaks under expansive crowns of cloud. The journey from Spiez along Lake Thun to Interlaken is like an elegant boat trip. Even though you're on dry land, you can almost hear the water lapping against the shiny wooden hull. Interlaken occupies an old alluvial plain at the transition to Lake Brienz, which is where we turn south towards Wilderswil. Cutting into the

HOTEL & RESTAURANT

HOTEL BELLEVUE DES ALPES
3801 KLEINE SCHEIDEGG
WWW.SCHEIDEGG-HOTELS.CH

DES ALPES

Jungfraujoch

LUZERN

Bei Sherlock-Holmes-Fans läuft hier sofort ein ganz eigenes Kopfkino ab, das nach einer gedachten Wanderung unterhalb des Mittelhorns drüben bei Meiringen an den Reichenbachfällen endet (Nachlesen? – Siehe: „Sherlock Holmes – Das letzte Problem").

Sherlock Holmes fans will immediately have their own mental picture of the place, ending after an imaginary hike at the Reichenbach Falls below the Mittelhorn near Meiringen (to bone up on the story check out "Sherlock Holmes – The Final Problem").

landfläche am Übergang zum Brienzer See eingerichtet, hier biegen wir nach Süden in Richtung Wilderswil ab. Schneiden ins Lütschinental hinein und dringen dann weiter nach Osten vor – das Ziel dieses Abstechers liegt in Grindelwald. Bei Sherlock-Holmes-Fans läuft hier sofort ein ganz eigenes Kopfkino ab, das nach einer gedachten Wanderung unterhalb des Mittelhorns drüben bei Meiringen an den Reichenbachfällen endet (Nachlesen? – Siehe: „Sherlock Holmes – Das letzte Problem").

Wer es nicht so mit Vorstellungskraft hat und sich trotzdem gruseln möchte, kann sich einfach gegenüber der Eiger-Nordwand eine Weile ins Gras setzen und das schwarze Ungetüm von senkrecht abfallender Wand ansehen, das da über Grindelwald aufragt. Man sieht diesem Berg an, dass er ein Killer ist.

Bis wir in Interlaken zurück sind, hat sich die Gänsehaut wieder etwas geglättet, jetzt geht es auf die letzten Kilometer dieser Mammutetappe vom äußersten Südwesten der Schweiz bis hierher ins Innere. Bei Giswil zielen wir hinüber ans nördliche Ufer des Sarnersees und fahren dann über die Glaubenbergstraße in Richtung Entlebuch. Karge Gebirgsriffe schneiden aus saftig grünen Matten, die Welt ist kleinteilig und still, die Abendsonne tüncht eine atemberaubend schöne Landschaft in Orange. Wir fahren schweigend und glücklich, Bilder brennen sich auf Netzhäute und ins Unterbewusstsein. In dieser Nacht, in Luzern am westlichen Ende des Vierwaldstättersees, träumen wir: von Aliens, finsteren Bergen und purer Schönheit.

Lütschinental Valley, we press on further east, as the final destination of this detour is in Grindelwald. Sherlock Holmes fans will immediately have their own mental picture of the place, ending after an imaginary hike at the Reichenbach Falls below the Mittelhorn near Meiringen (to bone up on the story check out "Sherlock Holmes – The Final Problem"). If you lack the necessary imaginative powers and still want a thrill, you can simply sit for a while on the grassy area opposite the north face of the Eiger and consider the black monster of the vertically sloping rock wall that looms ominously over Grindelwald. It's not hard to see that this mountain is a killer.

By the time we get back to Interlaken, our goose bumps have abated a little, so we can now contemplate the last few kilometers of this mammoth stage from the far southwest of Switzerland to the interior. At Giswil we head for the northern shore of Lake Sarnen and then drive the Glaubberg Pass road in the direction of Entlebuch. Barren mountain crags slash their way out of a lush green landscape. The world is fragmented and silent as the evening sun bathes a breathtakingly beautiful landscape in orange light. We drive on silently and happily, while images burn onto our retinas and into our subconscious. That night, in Lucerne at the western end of Lake Lucerne, we dream: of aliens, dark brooding mountains and pure beauty.

HOTEL & RESTAURANT

HOTEL BEAU SÉJOUR LUCERNE
HALDENSTRASSE 53
6006 LUZERN
WWW.BEAUSEJOURLUCERNE.CH

MARTIGNY LUZERN

Martigny liegt im Dreiländereck zwischen Schweiz, Italien und Frankreich. Hier, am beinahe südöstlichsten Punkt unserer Reise durch die Schweiz, fahren wir über den famosen Col de Champex bis zum Fuß des Grand Saint Bernard. Erst an der Passhöhe dieses 2.500 Meter hohen Bergpasses drehen wir mit einem Blick ins Aostatal ab. Der Weg führt uns zurück nach Martigny und dann weiter an der Rhône entlang in Richtung Genfersee. Abstecher in die angrenzenden Bergmassive von Les Diablerets oder zum Lac de l'Hongrin versüßen den Ritt nach Norden, in Richtung der Region Gruyère (Greyerz) streben wir dann weiter nach Norden. Lange Zeit bleiben wir im Tal der Saane und drehen dann nach Westen ab. Es geht nun über den Jaunpass bis ins Simmental, auf beinahe gerader Linie von West nach Ost. Nach dieser Fahrt durch die Kantone Wallis und Fribourg landen wir im Kanton Bern, hier erreichen wir nach vielen Kilometern im französischsprachigen Teil der Schweiz erneut die „schwyzerdütschen" Kantone. Von Spiez am Thunersee geht es nach Interlaken, hier muss ein Abstecher ins berühmte Grindelwald am Fuß der Eiger-Nordwand natürlich unbedingt sein. Nach einer Fahrt durch das UNESCO Biosphärenreservat Entlebuch erreichen wir in Luzern das Ziel der Etappe.

—

Martigny is located in the triangle between Switzerland, Italy and France. Here, at almost the most southerly point of our journey through Switzerland, we cross the famous Col de Champex to the foot of the Grand Saint Bernard. We wait until we reach the top of this 2,500 meter high mountain pass before turning to view the Aosta Valley. The path leads us back to Martigny and then further along the Rhône towards Lake Geneva. Detours to the nearby mountain massifs of Les Diablerets or to Lac de l'Hongrin are welcome rewards as we travel north toward the Gruyère region, after which we head further north again. We remain in the Saane valley for some time and then turn west. Then we cross the Jaun Pass to the Simmental Valley, following an almost straight line from west to east. After this trip through the cantons of Valais and Fribourg, we arrive in the canton of Bern, where, after many kilometers in the French-speaking part of Switzerland, we find ourselves once again in German-speaking territory. We travel from Spiez on Lake Thun to Interlaken, where we take a detour to the world-famous Grindelwald at the foot of the north face of the Eiger – a must. After a trip through the UNESCO World Heritage Site that is the Entlebuch Biosphere Reserve, we reach the end of this stage in Lucerne.

510 KM • 10 STUNDEN // 316 MILES • 10 HOURS

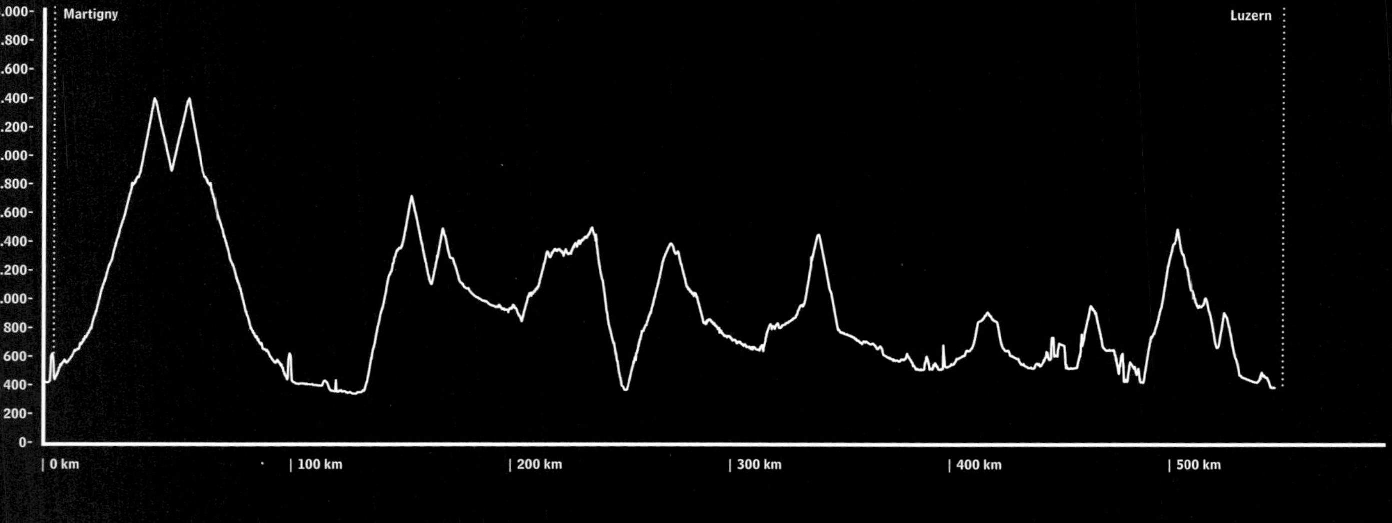

Solothurn
BIEL/BIENNE
BERN
KÖNIZ
FRIBOURG
THUN
Spiez
Burgdorf
Langnau
Interlaken
EMMEN
LUZERN
Sarnen
Zug
Martigny
SION
Sierre
Visp
Brig
Zermatt
Domodossola
VERBANIA
AOSTA

LUZERN
VALS

240 KM • 5 STUNDEN // 150 MILES • 6 HOURS

Vor Tausenden von Jahren ist die Zentralschweiz von einer mächtigen Eiskappe bedeckt. Dann, irgendwann, beginnen die Gletscher der Eiszeit sich zurückzuziehen. Dieses Verschwinden dauert in von Menschen fassbaren Zeiträumen unendlich, ungreifbar lange. Denken wir also einen Moment im Zeitraffer: Eis schmilzt, bildet mächtige Ströme, deren Nachfahren heute noch als die großen Flüsse Europas in die Nordsee und das Schwarze Meer fließen, schließlich beginnen sich von der Eislast der Gletscher befreite Berge zu heben, Land formt sich.

—

Thousands of years ago, Central Switzerland was covered by a mighty ice cap. Then, at some point, the Ice Age glaciers began to retreat. This process lasts indefinitely, covering intangibly long periods that are difficult for humans to grasp. So let's think for a moment in terms of a time-lapse film: ice melts, forming the mighty rivers, whose descendants still flow into the North Sea and the Black Sea as the great rivers of Europe. Mountains, finally freed from the icy weight of the glaciers, begin to rise and land is formed.

KLAUSEN-PASSHÖHE
KLAUSEN-PASSHÖHE
HOTEL

Und dann, am Ende dieses Prozesses (man müsste natürlich eher sagen: in der aktuellen Momentaufnahme eines immer noch andauernden Prozesses) bleibt von den Gletschern der Eiszeit nur noch eine Schmelzwasser-Lache im Tal zwischen den Bergen übrig. Die Lache ist groß, sehr groß: Beinahe 115 Quadratkilometer misst sie, hat mehrere Arme in diversen Tälern und sie ist 215 Meter tief. Ganz am Ende dieser Zeitraffer-Betrachtung taucht an ihrem westlichen Ende eine Stadt der Menschen auf: Luciaria. Lucerna. Luzern. Nach dieser Stadt und dem sie umgebenden Kanton gleichen Namens tauft man die Schmelzwasser-Lache den „Luzerner See". Allerdings ist Luzern nur ein Anrainer des Sees. Und weil die Schweizer streithaft sind, der stetig gelebte Ausgleich daher wichtig ist, bekommt unser Gletscherzungenbecken etwas später einen neuen Namen. Ganz pragmatisch: Vier Kantone der Schweiz treffen sich ungefähr in der Mitte des Sees, Kantone nannte man früher „Waldstätten", hier heißen sie Uri, Schwyz, Unterwalden, Luzern, und diese Vier teilen sich das Ufer ebenso wie die grüne Tiefe des Sees – des Vierwaldstättersees.

Und noch eine andere Geschichte spinnt sich am Ufer des Vierwaldstättersees: Auf einer zum See hin abfallenden Wiese bei Seelisberg sollen sich Vertreter der Kantone Uri, Schwyz und Unterwalden ungefähr im Herbst des Jahres 1307 getroffen haben, um ein Bündnis der bis dahin kaum miteinander verbundenen Orte der Zentralschweiz gegen die habsburgischen Fürsten aus dem heutigen Aargau einzugehen. Der Schwur auf der Rütliwiese gehört zum nationalen Identitätsinventar der Eidgenossenschaft, kein Mensch weiß wirklich ob und wie sich die Sache so oder anders oder überhaupt zugetragen hat, aber man kann es sich schon gut vorstellen: trotziges Aufbegehren gegen die transalpinen, europäischen Großmächte in einer schweizerischen Variante, während am anderen Seeufer harte Felsgipfel aus schroffem Vorgebirge ragen und der türkisgrüne See den Schwur wortlos beeidet. Ungefähr das ist die Welt, in der wir in unsere letzte Etappe starten: Aus Luzern kommend fahren wir am Südufer des Sees entlang, während weiße Schiffe übers Wasser ziehen und die Berge wieder einmal ganz alltägliche Dramatik inszenieren. Bei Stansstad geht es über die Brücke im Ausgang zum angegliederten Alpnacher See und dann bei Emmetten raus ans Rütli. Dort sitzen wir im Gras, Sonne leuchtet von einem azurblauen

And then, at the end of this process (which, of course, you would have to say is still ongoing in terms of our current perspective), all that remains of the glaciers of the Ice Age is a puddle of meltwater in the valley between the mountains. The pool is quite sizable, very sizable in fact: it measures almost 115 square kilometers, with several arms in various valleys and 215 meters deep. Almost at the very end of this time-lapse sequence, a city of people appears at the western end of the lake: Luciaria. Lucerna. Lucerne. The meltwater pool is named "Lake Lucerne" after the city and the surrounding canton of the same name. However, Lucerne is only one of the settlements on the lake. Because the Swiss are a quarrelsome lot, making it important to constantly seek balance, our many-armed glacier basin was given a new German name, "Vierwaldstättersee", a little later. It was quite a pragmatic solution really: four of Switzerland's cantons – Uri, Schwyz, Unterwalden and Lucerne – meet roughly in the middle of the lake, sharing the lake shore as well as the green depths of the lake. The old German word for these cantons was "Waldstätten", so Lake Lucerne's German name translates as "the lake of the four cantons".

Yet another tale is spun about the shores of Lake Lucerne: on a meadow near Seelisberg that slopes down towards the lake, known as the Rütliwiese, representatives of the cantons of Uri, Schwyz and Unterwalden are said to have met in autumn 1307 to form an alliance of these previously barely connected regions of central Switzerland against the Habsburg princes of what is modern day Aargau. The oath sworn on the Rütliwiese is an integral part of the national identity of the Swiss Confederation. No one really knows whether this really happened as reported or how the matter was decided one way or the other. Nevertheless, it's not hard to imagine it: a defiant Swiss rebellion against the great transalpine European powers, while on the other side of the lake, hard rocky peaks protrude from the rugged promontory and the turquoise-green lake in silent witness to the oath. This is roughly the world in which our final stage begins: approaching from Lucerne, we drive along the southern shore of the lake, while white ships drift across the water and the mountains stage a repeat performance of their daily drama. At Stansstad we cross the bridge at the exit for the adjoining Lake Alpnach and then at Emmetten we head for the Rütli. There we take some time out

Himmel, während über unseren Köpfen das weiße Kreuz auf rotem Grund sanft im Alpenwind flaggt. Unternehmungslustig machen wir uns dann wieder auf die Reise, wollen noch einmal diesem herrlichen Land huldigen. Am südöstlichsten Winkel des Vierwaldstättersees fließt die Reuss heran, ganz wichtig in ihrem breiten Schwemmlanddelta, sie scheint sich für ein Großereignis zu halten – dann sieht sie den mächtigen Urzeit-See und verschwindet kleinlaut in ihm. Wir springen über den Fluss und machen uns in Richtung Klausenpass davon. Langsam und stetig gewinnt die Straße im Tal an Höhe, klettert aus Wiesen immer weiter nach oben und wird zu einer Balkonstraße zwischen grantelnden Berg-Riffen mit steil abstürzenden Wänden und dem Tal tief unten. Nach langer Fahrt haben wir die Passhöhe erreicht, sind in der glasigen Luft unweit der Schneefelder und hochalpiner Kargheit angelangt. Wir schauen weit, können uns nicht sattsehen, schlendern lange auf der Passhöhe umher, bis die kalte Luft uns frösteln lässt.

Weiter geht es. In der Halbhöhenlage des Urnerbodens weit nach Osten und dann über zehn Serpentinen ins Tal der Linth hinunter. Glarus macht sich im Tal breit, und nach ein paar weiteren Kilometern nach Süden öffnet sich das Land in Richtung Zürichsee. Die Autobahn 3 trabt von Osten heran, als Exitstrategie aus den inneren Alpen hinaus. Hier geht die geschäftige, flache und moderne Schweiz los und hinter Zürich zieht der Rhein in Richtung Basel. Bis zum Rheinfall bei Schaffhausen lässt man ihn noch wild und romantisch sein, ab dann wird er zur Schifffahrtsstraße. Wir erinnern uns an den munteren, kleinen Bach in den Alpen und staunen über den mächtigen Strom, der dort oben nach Deutschland abbiegt und in wenigen Tagen träge und satt im Meer sein wird. Aber jetzt sind wir noch nicht reif für die Autobahnen nach Norden. Bei Mollis wechseln wir deshalb in die Hügel oberhalb des Walensees, der sich in die entgegengesetzte Richtung erstreckt: Weg vom offenen Land, hinein in die Berge der Kantone Glarus und Sankt Gallen. Eine freundliche Panoramastraße kurvt zwischen Walensee und Berg dahin, die passt jetzt perfekt zu unserer wehmütigen Stimmung auf den letzten

sitting on the grass, enjoying the sunshine and the azure blue sky. Above our heads the white cross on a red background gently flutters in the Alpine wind. Anxious to keep moving, we set off again, ready to pay homage to this wonderful country once more. The River Reuss flows into Lake Lucerne at its most south-eastern point. The broad alluvial delta seems to herald the arrival of a major waterway, however once the mighty prehistoric lake is in its sights, the Reuss just meekly disappears. We skip across the river and make our way towards the Klausen Pass. Slowly and steadily the road through the valley gains height, climbing further and further up from the meadows until you find yourself clinging to the sides of the grim mountain sides with their vertiginous walls and the valley deep below. After a long drive we reach the top of the pass, breathing in the crystalline air, almost within touching distance of the snow fields and high Alpine fastness. We gaze into the distance, unable to get our fill of the view, spending quite a long time walking around at the top of the pass until the cold air drives us back to the warm of our car.

On we go. We travel far to the east at a more modest height along the sides of the Urnerboden and then drop in ten serpentine bends to the valley of the River Linth. Glarus spreads itself out in the valley, and after a few more kilometers to the south the landscape opens up in the direction of Lake Zurich. Autobahn 3 approaches from the east, offering an exit strategy out of the inner Alps. This is where busy, modern, flat Switzerland begins and beyond Zurich the Rhine flows inexorably on towards Basel. The river remains wild and romantic until it reaches the Rhine Falls near Schaffhausen, where it becomes an inland shipping route. We remember the lively little brook we encountered in the Alps and marvel at the mighty torrent that now bends away toward Germany, growing sluggish and full as it reaches the sea in a few days' time. But we're not ready for the highways to the north. Therefore, at Mollis, we switch to the hills above Lake Walen, which extends in the opposite direction: away from the open country, into the mountains of the cantons of Glarus and Sankt Gallen. A welcoming panoramic route curves away between

Kilometern unserer Tour durch die Schweizer Alpen. Bei Quarten ist sie direkt am Seeufer gelandet, schiebt dann auf einen mächtigen Gebirgszug zu und wird durch dieses unüberwindliche Hindernis im Tal nach Südosten gezwungen: Von Walenstadt nach Flums, dann Mels und Sargans.

Was jetzt kommt, muss eigentlich nicht sein – aber irgendwie auch doch: Sich rüber ins Fürstentum Liechtenstein davonstehlen und dann bei Balzers in Richtung Sankt Luzisteig fahren. Die Straße hier hat einen überraschenden Backstage-Pass für die Schießanlagen der Kaserne am Luzisteigpass, den ständigen Tag-der-offenen-Tür hätte man der sonst so in sich gekehrten Schweizer Armee überhaupt nicht zugetraut. Die Straße zwängt sich durch ein schmales Nadelöhr-Tor alter Festungsanlagen, gleich darauf segelt man durch ein Waldstück und findet nach ein paar hundert Metern Fahrt, was man sucht – das Heidi-Land.

Denn mal ehrlich: Der innere Achtjährige in uns wollte doch schon immer mal nachsehen, ob es diese Alm-Öhi-Berghütte wirklich gibt. Und wie sie aussieht. Oberhalb von Bad Ragaz und Maienfeld geht das. Hier soll diese vermutlich berühmteste Geschichte der Schweiz passiert sein, am Fuß des Glegghorn. – Der Abstecher lohnt sich aber auch, wenn man einfach nur ein paar Kilometer Kurven hinlegen möchte, statt der Schnellstraßen-Zwangsetappe im Rheintal. Zuerst der Aufstieg von der Liechtensteiner Seite, dann das Hindurchschlüpfen im Bergwald und schließlich das herrliche Hinuntersegeln ins Rheintal zwischen Steinmäuerchen inmitten der Weinberge.

Ein wunderschöner, leichtfüßiger Spaß. Dann: Landquart, Chur, Flims, Laax, Ilanz. Plötzlich haben die Ortsnamen wieder diesen stolpernden rätoromanischen Zungenschlag. Und die Berge stehen enger, die Luft wird klarer, die Welt kleinteilig und herb. Lange schwingen wir mit der Straße bis ans Ende des Tals, bis sie in Vals endet. Mitten in den Alpen, mitten in der Schweiz. Am Ende der Reise. Am Beginn einer Neuen.

Lake Walen and the mountain, the perfect fit for our wistful mood as we complete the last kilometers of our tour of the Swiss Alps. At Quarten, the road lands directly on the lakeshore, before pushing towards a mighty mountain range, where it is forced southeast into the valley by this insurmountable solid obstacle: we drive from Walenstadt to Flums, then on to Mels and Sargans.

The next part of our journey isn't really essential, and yet it feels unmissable: we sneak away to the Principality of Liechtenstein and then drive to Balzers in the direction of Sankt Luzisteig. The road here affords a surprising backstage glimpse of the shooting range of the army barracks on the Luzisteig Pass and a chance to see the usually fairly secret might of the Swiss armed forces in action. The road squeezes its way through a narrow gap between old fortifications and immediately afterwards you find yourself cruising through a forest, where your search is finally rewarded after a few hundred meters – you've reached Heidi-Land.

After all, let's be honest, the eternal eight-year-old in all of us has always wanted to see whether Heidi's mountain hut really existed and what it looked like. Here, above Bad Ragaz and Maienfeld is your chance to find out. At the foot of the Glegghorn is the setting for "Heidi", probably the most famous story in Switzerland. – The detour is also worthwhile if you simply want to enjoy a few kilometers of curves instead of the obligatory expressway of the Rhine Valley. First we climb from the Liechtenstein side, then slip through the mountain forest and finally sail down into the Rhine Valley between vineyards and stone walls. What wonderful, fleet-footed fun.

Next come Landquart, Chur, Flims, Laax and Ilanz. The place names are once again redolent of the awkward sounds of the Romansh language. The mountains draw closer together, the air grows clearer and the world becomes smaller and more austere. We follow the road for some time to the end of the valley until we reach Vals. We've arrived at the middle of the Alps and the center of Switzerland. This is the end of our trip. And the beginning of a new one.

HOTELS

7132 HOTEL
7132 VALS
WWW.7132.COM

BRÜCKE 49
7132 VALS
WWW. BRUCKE49.CH

THERME VALS

LUZERN VALS

Luzern ist eine Fahrpause wert, man muss es ganz klar sagen. Die Kantonshauptstadt im Westen des Vierwaldstättersees lockt mit einer sehenswerten Mischung aus neuzeitlicher Moderne und mittelalterlicher Atmosphäre, es gibt viel zu sehen. Für die Fahrt entlang des Vierwaldstättersees gilt das genauso: Der See liegt größtenteils so atemberaubend dicht ins Tal gepackt, dass die Straße sich entweder in gewundenen Felsgalerien und Tunnelpassagen wiederfindet oder überhaupt nicht direkt ans Seeufer gelangt. Gelegentlich wirkt das beinahe wie ein skandinavischer Fjord, die vielen Nebentäler und Windungen des großen Sees tragen zusätzlich zur magischen Stimmung bei. Gleichzeitig ballt sich Schweizer Geschichte rund um den See – wer hier etwas Hintergrundwissen gesammelt hat, fährt auch noch durch eine unsichtbare Wolke von eidgenössischen Legenden. Über den Klausenpass verlassen wir die Gegend um den Vierwaldstättersee in östlicher Richtung, die Fahrt ins Tal der Linth streckt sich weit und dauert ohne Pausen bereits rund eine Stunde. Über Glarus stoßen wir dann weiter bis zum Walensee vor, rollen in herrlicher Panoramalage entlang des Südufers nach Osten und auf Sargans zu. Hier, im Rheintal, sollten Heidi-Fans unbedingt einen Abstecher in die Gegend um Maienfeld und Bad Ragaz unternehmen, für alle anderen geht es den Flusslauf hinauf über Chur bis Reichenau. Mit dem Vorderrhein erreichen wir Ilanz und fahren dann dem Etappenende bei Vals entgegen.

—

We must admit that it is worth taking a break from driving to explore Lucerne. The cantonal capital in the western part of Lake Lucerne attracts visitors for its mixture of modernity and medieval atmosphere. It is certainly well worth as visit as there is so much to see. The same is true of the drive along Lake Lucerne: the lake is for the most part packed so tightly into the valley that the road either follows winding rock galleries and tunnels or remains a long way from the lakeshore. Occasionally it almost looks like a Scandinavian fjord, the many side valleys and winding inlets of the huge lake adding to the magical atmosphere. Switzerland's history is also concentrated around the lake and, armed with a little background knowledge, you can find yourself driving through an invisible cloud of Swiss legends. We leave the area around Lake Lucerne in an easterly direction via the Klausen Pass. The journey into the Linth Valley is a long one and takes around an hour without stops. We then move on via Glarus to Lake Walen, where we follow a wonderful panoramic route along the south bank to the east towards Sargans. Here, in the Rhine Valley, Heidi fans should definitely take a detour to the area around Maienfeld and Bad Ragaz. Everyone else should head up river via Chur to Reichenau. Joining the Vorderrhein, we reach Ilanz and then drive to the end of the stage in Vals.

240 KM • 5 STUNDEN // 150 MILES • 6 HOURS

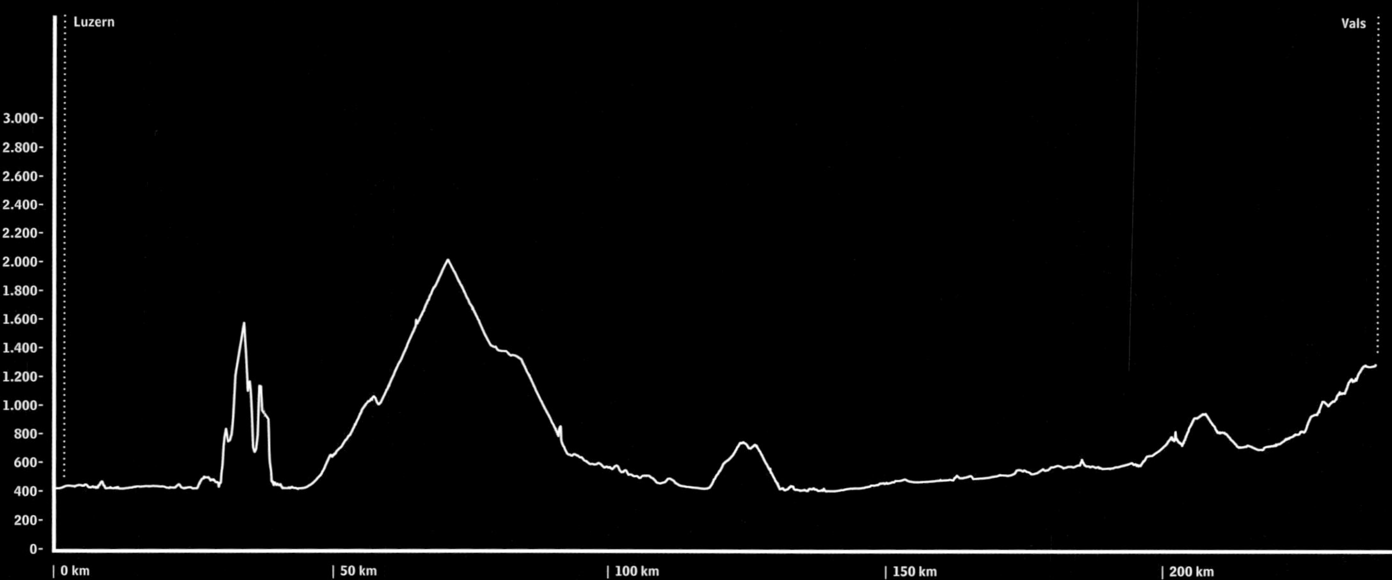

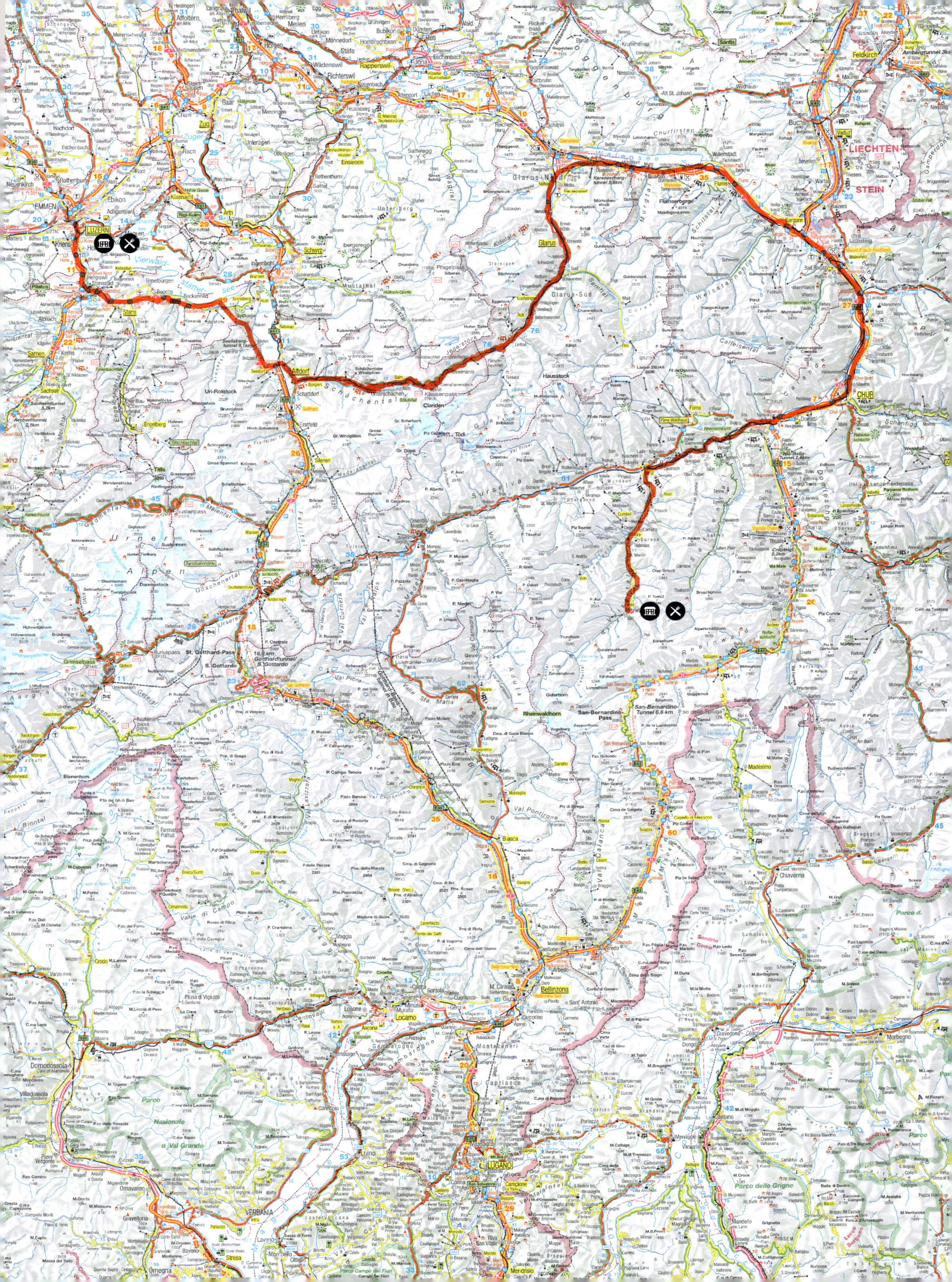

LUZERN
Zug
Schwyz
Altdorf
Glarus
Chur
LIECHTEN-
STEIN
Vaduz
Bellinzona
Locarno
Lugano
Domodossola
Verbania
Biasca
Rapperswil
Horgen
Stäfa
Einsiedeln
Sargans
Bad Ragaz
Flims
Ilanz
Disentis
Andermatt
Airolo
St. Gotthard-Pass
Grimselpass
Sustenpass
Klausenpass
Oberalppass
San-Bernardino-Pass
Thusis
Chiavenna
Menaggio
Mendrisio
Campione
Cannobio
Ascona

240
200
170
150

HEUER

MECHANICAL STOPWATCH
INK POINTER STOPWATCH
MECHANICAL STOPWATCH
MECHANICAL STOPWATCH

HEUER
CAL.11
SEVENTEEN
17 JEWELS
UNADJUSTED
SWISS

WORTH A VISIT: TAG HEUER

Und dann wäre da ja noch diese Stadt im Jura, rund 50 Kilometer westlich von Bern und in der luftigen Höhe von 1.000 Metern gelegen: La Chaux-de-Fonds. Hier im Westen der Schweiz hat sich eine Industrie eingerichtet, die auf das gesamte Land abstrahlt: Uhren.

Die wohl größten Erfindungen der Uhrenfertigung stammen aus dieser Region, Manufakturen und Marken mit Namen wie Donnerhall haben hier ihren Sitz. Zu diesen Superstars der Uhrenfertigung gehört TAG Heuer: 1860 in Saint-Imier gegründet, sitzt das Unternehmen heute in der Uhrenmetropole La Chaux-de-Fonds – die Stadt ist übrigens auch Geburtsort der Herren Louis Chevrolet und Le Corbusier, um an dieser Stelle den Spannungsbogen etwas weiter zu ziehen ... Wenn es aber um die Sekundenbruchteile des Unterwegsseins geht, darf man bei TAG Heuer durchaus die Zeit anhalten und ins Museum der legendären Zeitmesser-Marke verschwinden: „360°" heißt es, in seinem Allerheiligen aus Beton, Glas und tiefschwarzem Corian präsentiert TAG Heuer rund 300 Exemplare der wichtigsten Uhren aus der Firmengeschichte – wir sagen nur Carrera, Aquaracer, Steve McQueens Monaco ... „Techniques d'Avant Garde Heuer" ist eine Ikone der ganz rasanten Zeitmessung. Heuer hat in der Vergangenheit die Zeitnahme bei den olympischen Spielen verantwortet, während TAG Heuer unter anderem in der Formel E die letzte Kontrolle über einen Sport hat, in dem Zehntel- und Hundertstelsekunden zählen.

Absolute Präzision, höchste Qualität, hartnäckiger Erfindergeist, gewachsen auf dem kargen Boden einer Gebirgs-Hochebene – auch das ist die Schweiz. Und TAG Heuer 360° genau deshalb ganz bestimmt: Worth A Visit.

Let's not forget this city in the Jura mountains, around 50 kilometers west of Bern and located at the lofty heights of 1,000 meters above sea level: La Chaux-de-Fonds. Here, in the west of Switzerland, an industry has grown up that is known across the entire country: watchmaking.

Probably the greatest innovations in watchmaking come from this region. Manufacturers and brands with fantastic reputations are based here. TAG Heuer is one of these watchmaking superstars: founded in Saint-Imier in 1860, the company is now located in La Chaux-de-Fonds, one of the most famous cities of Swiss watch production. By the way, this is also the birthplace of Louis Chevrolet and Le Corbusier, which somehow seems to make perfect sense... If you're interested in learning more about how time is measured in fractions of a second, the museum of the legendary TAG Heuer brand is definitely a place to stop the clock and take the opportunity to admire its wonders: "360°" is the motto in the Holy of Holies, built from concrete, glass and deep black Corian, where TAG Heuer presents around 300 examples of the most important watches from the company's history – Carrera, Aquaracer, Steve McQueen's Monaco... "Techniques d'Avant Garde Heuer" is an icon among cutting-edge chronometers. Heuer used to provide the timepieces for the Olympics, while TAG Heuer is still the official timekeeper of Formula E, among other events, exercising the final say in sports where tenths and hundredths of a second count.

Absolute precision, top quality, determined inventiveness, growing from the barren soil of a high mountain plateau – that's Switzerland too. And the TAG Heuer 360° – definitely worth a visit.

Marlboro
parmalat
parmalat
JEB'S

31410

CARRERA
CALIBRE 16

TAG HEUER

55
MONTE-

MONACO
HEUER
AUTOMATIC
CHRONOGRAPH
28

Marlboro
parmalat
parmalat

SWISS

PASADENA PVD

ASK THE LOCAL

Jan Karl Baedeker (1979) schreibt über Automobilkultur, Reise, Architektur und Design. Er ist langjähriger Chefredaktor und Kreativchef des Magazins «Classic Driver» und Autor zahlreicher Bücher, unter anderem «Porsche Drive – Pass Portrait» und «Porsche Unseen». Zuletzt hat er mit Stefan Bogner den Bildband «Mountain Roads» herausgebracht. Jan lebt in Zürich und verbringt so viel Zeit wie möglich in den Bergen.

–

Jan Karl Baedeker (1979) writes about cars, travel, architecture and design. For many years he has been editor-in-chief and creative director of "Classic Driver" magazine and is the author of numerous books, including "Porsche Drive – Pass Portrait" and "Porsche Unseen". He recently published the photo book "Mountain Roads" in collaboration with Stefan Bogner. Jan lives in Zurich and spends as much time as possible in the mountains.

Baedeker? – Irgendwie kommt einem der Name bekannt vor. Oder täuscht das? Mein Ur-Ur-Großvater Karl Baedeker hat vor fast 200 Jahren ein Medien-Startup gegründet und ziemlich disruptive Reisehandbücher herausgebracht. Damals hatte gerade das Dampfschiff die Kutsche abgelöst, die Eisenbahn wurde auch gerade aufgegleist – und die neuen «Schnellreisenden» wollten wissen, welche Sehenswürdigkeiten man unbedingt gesehen haben muss, in welchem Gasthof man über den Tisch gezogen wird und wie viele Flaschen Cognac man auf eine Gipfelbesteigung mitzunehmen hat. Die kleinen roten Reiseführer waren im 19. und 20. Jahrhundert ziemlich erfolgreich. Mein Großvater und mein Vater waren die letzten Verleger aus der Familie – aber ein bisschen Fernweh steckt mir wohl auch in den Knochen.

Einmal quer über die Alpen: Landkarte oder Navigationssystem? Landkarte. Da gibt es keine Staus, keine Straßensperren und keine berechnete Zeit bis zum Ziel. Oder die ehrliche Antwort?

Top Five deiner Schweizer Alpenpässe? Gotthard, der Epische. Susten, der Cinematografische. Grimsel, der Sublime. Flüela, die Schneepiste. Albis, der Kleine für die Mittagspause.

Und die Top Five deiner Porsche, die perfekt zu diesen Pässen passen? Immer die besonders kleinen, leichten und puristischen Porsche. Early 911S, 914/6, 964 Carrera RS, Boxster 718 Spyder, 904 Living Legend. Je nach Wetter und Saison.

Was macht den Schweizer in dir aus? Ich hoffe: Gelassenheit, Ausgewogenheit, Freude an Qualität, Ästhetik, Understatement. Ich fürchte: Überpünktlichkeit, Perfektionismus, Ernsthaftigkeit.

Taschenmesser, Absinth, das Tourbillon, Rickenbacker-E-Gitarren, Heidi, Instantcafé, LSD … – welche Schweizer Erfindung ist deiner Meinung nach die allergrößte? Also Albert Hofmann sollte eigentlich den 100-Franken-Schein schmücken – oder noch besser: die Bundesbriefmarke. Aber im Ernst, die allergrößte Schweizer Erfindung ist entweder der Reißverschluss oder das World Wide Web.

Nur drei Tage Zeit – wo muss man dann in der Schweiz unbedingt gewesen sein? Nur drei Tage Zeit? Das muss ein gestresster Deutscher sein. Also erstmal runterkommen und in der Therme Vals von Peter Zumthor brutalistisch durchblubbern lassen, dann im Holzkokon von Tadao

Baedeker? – That name sounds kind of familiar. Why is that? My great-great-grandfather, Karl Baedeker founded a media start-up company almost 200 years ago and published travel guides that set new standards. At that time, the steamship had just replaced the horse-drawn carriage and trains were in their infancy. Back then, "fast-paced travelers" wanted to know which sights they shouldn't miss, where to eat without getting ripped off and how many bottles of cognac you would need for a summit ascent. The little red travel guides were very successful in the 19th and 20th centuries. My grandfather and father were the last publishers in the family – but I guess I have been bitten by the travel bug too.

When crossing the Alps do you use a map or a GPS system? Map. There are no traffic jams, no road blocks and no calculated time of arrival. Or would you prefer the honest answer?

Your top five Alpine passes in Switzerland? The Gotthard, the epic Susten, the cinematic Grimsel, the sublime Flüela, the snow-covered Albis – perfect for a short crossing in your lunch break.

And your top five Porsches to match these passes? I always go for particularly small, light and purist Porsches. Early 911S, 914/6, 964 Carrera RS, Boxster 718 Spyder, 904 Living Legend. It all depends on the weather and season.

What is it that makes you particularly Swiss? I would hope the answer would be: calmness, balance, an eye for quality, aesthetics, understatement. However I'm afraid the real truth is: over-punctuality, perfectionism, seriousness.

The penknife, absinthe, the tourbillon, Rickenbacker electric guitars, Heidi, instant coffee, LSD… – which Swiss invention is the greatest in your opinion? I believe Albert Hofmann's face should be on the 100 Swiss franc note – or even better the stamps. But seriously, the greatest Swiss invention of all is either the zip fastener or the World Wide Web.

Let's say I have only three days – what should I not miss in Switzerland? Just three days? Sounds like a stressed-out German to me. So first take the pace down by spending some time in Peter Zumthor's brutalist Therme Vals spa complex, then gaze out of the large windows into the mist-filled mountains from the wooden cocoon designed by Tadao Ando until your head is clear and your heart rate

Ando aus dem Großformatfenster in die nebligen Berge blicken, bis der Kopf wieder angenehm leer und der Puls auf Niederfrequenz ist. Am nächsten Tag dann die große Hafenrundfahrt der Bündner Alpen über Splügen, Chiavenna, Maloja, St. Moritz, Julier, Albula, um pünktlich zum Fünf-Uhr-Tee mit Orchester im Waldhaus in Sils Maria zu sitzen. Am nächsten Morgen Wecker auf halb sechs zur zweiten Passrunde via Ofenpass, Stelvio, Umbrail, Reschen. Lunch im verwunschenen Garten des Hotels Piz Linard in Lavin. Danach noch rasch ins Muzeum Susch und via Flüelapass zurück ins Flachland. Das Wochenende bei einem Absacker in der Kronenhalle Bar in Zürich soigniert ausfaden lassen.

Wenn es die Schweiz nicht gäbe – weshalb müsste man sie dann erfinden? Einen durch Kontinentalplattencrash entstandenen alpinen, kosmopolitischen Abenteuerspielplatz mit Schckoladenfabriken braucht einfach jeder bewohnbare Planet.

Was ist typisch Schweizerisch? Das nüchtern-sachliche Grafik-Plakat im «Weltformat» mit seinen 128 × 90,5 Zentimetern. War für mich ein Grund zu bleiben.

Fondue oder Birchermüesli? Natürlich beides.

Luftgekühlt oder wassergekühlt? Das Müesli?

Elektroautos sind … verdammt schnell. Und verdammt spannend, wenn bei der Berg- und Talfahrt plötzlich die Reichweite abfällt und man im Kopf die maximal mögliche Bremskraftrückgewinnung bis zur einzigen Schnellladestation im Kanton berechnen.

Ein Song über dich hätte folgenden Titel: … «He ate and ate and never gained weight» vom experimentellen welschen Elektrokollektiv Moitié-Moitié.

Welche Rolle in welchem bekannten Film hättest du gerne gespielt? Ich gehe lieber hinter der Kamera in Deckung als davor zu stehen. Wenn ich vom Film träume, dann von der Arbeit mit großen Regisseuren wie Stanley Kubrick, Werner Herzog, Chris Marker. Als Antonioni für «Blow Up» den Londoner Maryon Park grün färben ließ, wäre ich wahnsinnig gerne dabei gewesen – wenn auch nur mit einem Eimer voll Farbe.

Und wenn ein Film über dich gedreht würde, welcher Schauspieler müsste deine Rolle übernehmen? John Malkovich.

has slowed to normal. The next day should be spent on a tour of the Graubünden Alps via the Splügen, Chiavenna, Maloja, St. Moritz, Julier and Albula Passes, arriving in time for five o'clock tea to the sound of the orchestra in the Waldhaus in Sils Maria. The next morning, rise to your alarm clock at half past five for a second session on the Alpine passes: the Ofen, Stelvio, Umbrail and Reschen. Enjoy lunch in the enchanting gardens of the Hotel Piz Linard in Lavin. Then move quickly on to the Muzeum Susch contemporary art museum and finally back to the plains via the Flüela Pass. Bring the weekend to a gentle close with a nightcap in the Kronenhalle Bar in Zurich.

If Switzerland didn't exist, why would we need to invent it? Every inhabitable planet needs an alpine, cosmopolitan adventure playground full of chocolate factories created by the collision of continental tectonic plates.

What is typically Swiss? The universal use of "Weltformat"-sized posters, measuring 128 x 90.5 centimeters. This was certainly a reason for me to stay.

Fondue or müesli? Both, of course.

Air-cooled or water-cooled? Are we still talking about müesli?

Electric cars are… damn fast. And damn exciting when the range suddenly drops while you're driving in the mountains and you have to work out in your head the maximum possible braking force recovery before you reach the only rapid charging station in the canton.

If someone wrote a song about you, what would the title be? "He ate and ate and never gained weight" by the Swiss experimental electronic music collective Moitié-Moitié.

Which role in which famous film would you have liked to have played? I'd prefer to stay behind the camera than stand in front of it. If I think about film, then I dream of working with great directors like Stanley Kubrick, Werner Herzog or Chris Marker. When Antonioni had London's Maryon Park dyed green for "Blow Up", I'd have loved to be there – even if only to carry a bucket full of paint.

And if a film were made about you, which actor would play you? John Malkovich.

Hotel
zur Sonne
Wirtschaft
Speiserestaurant

BACKSTAGE

Moment mal, sagen CURVES-Leser der ersten Ausgaben, CURVES unterwegs in der Schweiz, das gab es doch bereits? – Klare Antwort: Richtig. In die Schweiz hat es CURVES schon einmal verschlagen. Und die versteckte Wahrheit ist: Sogar noch viel öfter. Beinahe hätten wir jetzt gesagt „unzählige Male" oder „wir haben aufgehört zu zählen".

Aber eben das stimmt nun wirklich nicht. Wir können uns an jedes Mal erinnern, an jeden gefahrenen Meter. Sogar als wir Kinder waren und mit an Seitenscheiben plattgedrückten Nasen in den Autos unserer Eltern in die Schweiz hineingefahren sind, ist eine bunte und lebendige Erinnerung für uns. Dieser erhabene Schock, wenn sich aus den Hügeln der Voralpen auf einmal gigantische Berge schälen, die wenig später das im Tal dahingleitende Auto umzingeln und mit wolkenverhangenen Steilwänden oder in der Sonne gleißenden Schneegipfeln über einem thronen. „Da sind die Berge", sagt man dann andächtig und der Kopf geht in den

Some of the CURVES readers who have been with us from the start will ask "Hasn't CURVES covered Switzerland already?" – The obvious answer is, yes, CURVES has been to Switzerland once before. The real truth is we've been there even more often. We almost said "countless times" or "we stopped counting", but that wouldn't really be true.

We can remember every visit and every meter driven, even when we were kids and accompanied our parents to Switzerland, our noses pressed flat against the windows of the car. These are colorful and vivid memories for us. How could we forget the sublime shock when gigantic mountains suddenly rose up from the foothills of the Alps, surrounding our car a little later as we cruised through the valleys, gazing down on us from cloud-covered steep walls or snowy peaks glistening in the sun. "These mountains are really something," we murmured reverently as our heads tilted back in amazement and we felt the goosebumps running from the back of ours

HOTEL
GLETSCHER-RESTAURANT
BELVEDERE

Nacken, man staunt und spürt eine kleine Gänsehaut, die sich von den Schultern in die Arme zieht. Selbstverständlich wissen wir es heute, als Erwachsene, besser, aber als Kinder haben wir gespürt, dass Berge Persönlichkeiten sind. Manche freundlich und weise oder gemütlich und humorvoll, andere ungestüm und tückisch. Götter wohnen auf den Bergen – so viel steht fest, wenn du acht Jahre alt bist und aus dem Autofenster schaust. Es kommt einem dann unerhört vor, dass Mutter und Vater mit diesem Auto tatsächlich hinauffahren, zu den Pässen und Almen. Etwas anmaßend, aber auch prickelnd. Oben steigst du dann aus, eben war es im Tal noch sonnig und warm, aber jetzt pfeift dir ein kalter Bergwind um die Nase. Schneefelder senden eisige Strahlen auf deine Haut, Murmeltiere pfeifen und Wolken jagen über einen Himmel, der sich nicht entscheiden kann, ob er blau und weit sein will, oder grau und drückend. Da stehst du dann, schaust nach unten und fragst dich, wie es sein kann, dass Menschen hier heraufkommen. Dürfen die das? Einfach so? Und wie geht das überhaupt? – Dann siehst du die Straße. Sie wirkt so zierlich und eifrig, wie sie aus dem Tal da unten emporsteigt. Sich in dichten Windungen am Sockel des Bergs anschleicht und dann als feiner Pinselstrich im Braun und Grün der Matten dahinstrebt.

Manchmal verschwindet sie aus der Sicht, dann taucht sie wieder auf und kämpft sich immer näher. Wird größer und größer und plötzlich verstehst du beim Anblick der mächtigen Stützmauer nur ein paar Meter weiter unter dir, dass eine Straße in den Bergen ein Kunstwerk ist. Ein Ausdruck der Gewalt und gleichzeitig der Demut: Menschen haben das Gebirge gebändigt, ihm ihre asphaltierten Zügel angelegt und einen Weg gebahnt – aber am Ende ist dieses Bauwerk lediglich geduldet. Wenn man dem Berg und seinen Launen nur lange genug Zeit lässt, wird die Straße wieder verschwinden. Bröckelnd, zerfallend, abrutschend. Sie ist eine Momentaufnahme – genau wie der Berg, zu dem sie jetzt gehört. Dieses Bild der Straße geht mit dir und für uns war es der Beginn von CURVES. Er liegt in den Bergen der Schweiz. Als Erinnerung an Serpentinen, an ihre Geometrie und statische Kraft. Später sind wir dann selbst in die Berge gefahren, haben diese andere Energie entdeckt, die pure Dynamik des Fahrens. Kurven. Tanzen. Sein. Soulful Driving eben. Auch das hat uns die Schweiz gelehrt.

Von hier bis zum letzten Schritt in unser CURVES-Abenteuer lag dann nur noch das Erwachen für die Welt und ihre Schichten aus Kultur und Wildheit, aus Geschichte, aus Werden und Vergehen. Kinder haben einen Nerv für all das, aber keine Worte. Die Freundlichkeit der Schweiz, ihre Schönheit und Tiefe sind immer mit uns gefahren, aber es hat lange gedauert, bis wir sie verstanden haben. Die stille Magie des Engadin oder die energiegeladene Vielschichtigkeit der Zentralschweiz. Am Ende steht also eine persönliche Beziehung, die wir zu diesem Land und

neck and down our arms. Of course we know better now as adults, but as children we felt that the mountains had personalities of their own. Some were friendly and wise, while others were playful and humorous, or impetuous and treacherous. When you are eight years old and looking out the car window, you're left in no doubt: the gods live in the mountains. It felt a bit presumptuous of your mom and dad to drive up to the passes and mountain pastures in their car. This feeling was also tinged with excitement. You would get out at the top, noticing that it had been sunny and warm in the valley just minutes ago, but up here a cold mountain wind whistled around your nose. The reflected sunshine from the snow fields pierced your skin. Marmots called to each other and clouds chased across a sky that could not make up its mind whether it wanted to be blue and wide or gray and oppressive. You stood there, looking down and wondering why would people come up here? Is this allowed? Just like that? And how does that even work? – Then you caught sight of the road.

It looked so delicate and eager as it rose from the valley below, sneaking up from the base of the mountain in tight turns and then pushing forward in thin brushstrokes through the brown and green vegetation. Sometimes it disappeared from view, only to reappear, working its way closer and closer. It got bigger and bigger and suddenly, when you saw the mighty retaining wall just a few meters below, you realized that a road through the mountains is a work of art. It is simultaneously an act of violence and humility: people have tamed the mountains, harnessing them with their asphalt reins. But in the end, nature only barely tolerates such constructions. If you were to allow the mountains enough time, the road would disappear again. It would crumble and slip away. So the road is just a snapshot in time – just like the mountain to which it now belongs. This understanding of the road stays with you and for us it was where CURVES was born: there in the mountains of Switzerland, a constant reminder of the geometry and static power of serpentine bends. Later we drove into the mountains ourselves, discovering this different energy, the pure dynamics of driving. Curving. Dancing. Being. Simply soulful driving. Switzerland taught us that too.

From here to the most recent step along the way of our CURVES adventure required an awakening to the world and its myriad layers of culture, history, untamed growth and decay. Children have a sense of all of this, but lack the words to express it. The welcoming friendliness of Switzerland, its beauty and depth have always been with us, but it took us a long time to understand the quiet magic of the Engadin or the energetic complexity of Central Switzerland. Thus, we have a personal relationship with this country and its landscapes. Sometimes we think about our journeys in a kind of bird's eye view.

TI 52356

S PL 3277

Die Freundlichkeit der Schweiz, ihre Schönheit und Tiefe sind immer mit uns gefahren, aber es hat lange gedauert, bis wir sie verstanden haben. Die stille Magie des Engadin oder die energiegeladene Vielschichtigkeit der Zentralschweiz. Am Ende steht also eine persönliche Beziehung, die wir zu diesem Land und seinen Landschaften haben. Manchmal denken wir in einer Art Vogelperspektive über unsere Fahrten nach, dann wird alles zu einer Art Modelleisenbahn-Miniaturlandschaft – und irgendwie ist die Schweiz das ja auch: so viel Fülle auf so wenig Raum.

The welcoming friendliness of Switzerland, its beauty and depth have always been with us, but it took us a long time to understand the quiet magic of the Engadin or the energetic complexity of Central Switzerland. Thus, we have a personal relationship with this country and its landscapes. Sometimes we think about our journeys in a kind of bird's eye view. That's when everything becomes a kind of model railway miniature landscape – and in a way Switzerland is that too: so much abundance in so little space.

seinen Landschaften haben. Manchmal denken wir in einer Art Vogelperspektive über unsere Fahrten nach, dann wird alles zu einer Art Modelleisenbahn-Miniaturlandschaft – und irgendwie ist die Schweiz das ja auch: so viel Fülle auf so wenig Raum. Vom Osten bei Österreich bis zum Westen an der Grenze nach Frankreich fährt man in wenigen Stunden, gefühlt dauert es aber Jahre, bis man sich durch all die Schichten und Kulturen und Wetterwechsel und Emotionen geträumt hat. Das Bild der Miniaturlandschaft greift dann schon nicht mehr, denn dann bist du bereits mittendrin in dieser reichen, weiten und überlebensgroßen Welt.

Dies ist also die Geschichte unserer Liebe zur Schweiz und weshalb wir immer wieder hierher zurückkommen: Unzählige Male sind wir hier gereist oder haben Autos auf den Bergstraßen fotografiert. Weil es so unvergleichlich gut passt. Auch auf dieser CURVES-Reise hatten wir mit dem Porsche 911 GT3 einen famosen Serpentinen-Surfer dabei und das hat uns zu einem Movie-Clip inspiriert, den man auf der CURVES-Webseite (www.curves-magazin.com) erleben kann. Mit einem Surf-Song als Soundtrack. Weil die besten Straßen-Wellen eben in der Schweiz zu finden sind und Porsche für uns die vermutlich besten „Surfbretter" für die Schweizer Alpen baut. Danke an Porsche! – Und ein lässiges „Hang Loose" geht raus an die Crew des 911 ST 2.5 Toadhall Racing, der 1972 Le Mans gerockt hat, fast 50 Jahre später mit uns die Schweiz. Mike, Marco und Marco: Danke fürs Mitfahren. Danke, 356, und natürlich: Grüezi, Schweiz. Wir sehen uns ganz bestimmt wieder.

That's when everything becomes a kind of model railway miniature landscape – and in a way Switzerland is that too: so much abundance in so little space. You can drive from the east near Austria to the west on the border with France in just a few hours, but it feels like it takes years before you have dreamed your way through all the layers and cultures and weather changes and emotions. That's when the image of a miniature landscape stops working, because then you are actually in the middle of a rich, wide world that is larger than life.

This is the story of our love affair with Switzerland and why we keep coming back here: we have been here countless times, photographing cars on the mountain roads because the country is such a good fit. On this CURVES trip, we once again had the pleasure of driving a famous serpentine surfer in the shape of the Porsche 911 GT3, which inspired us to make a movie clip for you to watch on the CURVES website (www.curves-magazin.com). Naturally we chose a surf song as the soundtrack. After all, the best road curls are found in Switzerland and Porsche probably builds the best "surfboards" for the Swiss Alps. Thank you Porsche! – We'd also like to say a casual "Hang Loose" to the crew of the 911 ST 2.5 Toadhall Racing, which rocked Le Mans in 1972 and still had enough gas in the tank to rock Switzerland with us almost 50 years later. Mike, Marco and Marco, thanks for coming with us.

Thank you, 356, and of course: Grüezi, Switzerland. We'll definitely see you again.

41
Toad Hall
CIBIE

FRANÇOIS HALARD
STOP PAINTING

ONDITOREI HANSELMAN

ovomaltin
DRINK
ovomaltine
CRUNCHY

rivella

Hospiz
St. Bernhardin
GASTHAUS RESTAURANT
WC
ECURIE
Robert BUCHET

S PL 3277

Nikon D850
NORD

Quartier
des
Generalissimus
SUWOROF
am 25 September
1799

HELIBERNINA.ch

S PL 3277

zum schwarzen Bären

SMC
CRESTA RUN

BERNINA BIER
CALANDA

Wössner
PIRELLI
TI·52356

GARASCHA BOTT SA
Serviceannahme

FURKA & GRIMSEL PASS

EFG BANK
5 26
TOTAL

S PL 3277

S PL 3277

Shell
CIBIE
41
Toad Hall
CIBIE

R. BUCHET
CIBIE

DE CARBON
PORSCHE

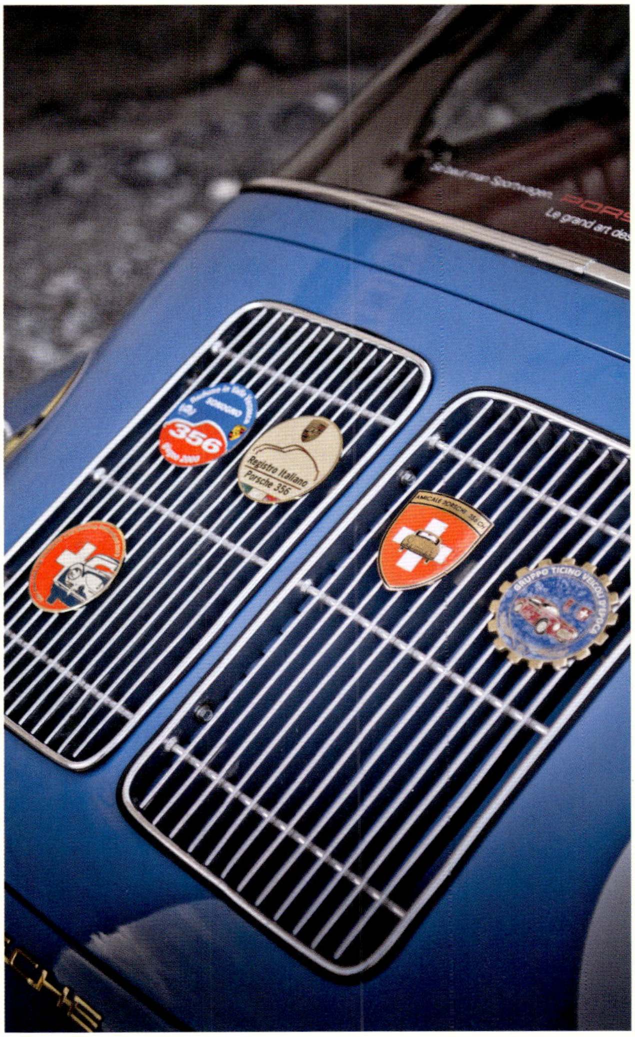
356
Registro Italiano
Porsche 356

Flüelen

41

S PL 3277

S PL 3277

R. BUCHET

HOTEL
GRIMSEL HOSPIZ

41
Toad Hall
CIBIE

S PL 3277

S PL 3277

DANK AN / THANKS TO
Bastian Schramm, Maximilian Ramisch, Ben Winter, Nadja Kneissler, Axel Gerber, Hanno Vienken, Michael Dorn, Michaela Bogner

SPECIAL FX / SPECIAL FX
Helibernina, Daniele Perfetti, Mike Gnani, Marco Halter, Marco & Chantal Pelucca, David Steca, Phil Gordon, Philipp Hohenthanner, Fabrizio D'Aloisio, Carolin Schmid, Porsche Schweiz, TAG Heuer

You are very welcome to visit us:

Porsche Classic Zentrum Genf
Impasse Colombelle 2
1218 Le Grand-Saconnex, Schweiz

Porsche Studio Zürich
Dufourstrasse 182/188
8008 Zürich, Schweiz

Porsche 911 GT3
Kraftstoffverbrauch kombiniert in l/100 km: 13,3-12,4 (NEFZ), 13,0-12,9 (WLTP);
CO_2-Emission in g/km kombiniert: 304-283 (NEFZ), 294-293 (WLTP), Stand 10/2021

Fuel consumption combined in l/100km: 13,3-12,4 (NEDC), 13,0-12,9 (WLTP);
CO_2 emissions combined in g/km: 304-283 (NEDC), 294-293 (WLTP); as of 10/2021

IMPRESSUM / IMPRINT

HERAUSGEBER/
PUBLISHER: CURVES MAGAZIN
THIERSCHSTRASSE 25
D-80538 MÜNCHEN

VERANTWORTLICH FÜR
DEN HERAUSGEBER/
RESPONSIBLE FOR
PUBLICATION:
STEFAN BOGNER

KONZEPT/CONCEPT:
STEFAN BOGNER
THIERSCHSTRASSE 25
D-80538 MÜNCHEN
SB@CURVES-MAGAZIN.COM

DELIUS KLASING
CORPORATE PUBLISHING
SIEKERWALL 21
D-33602 BIELEFELD

REDAKTION/
EDITORIAL CONTENT:
STEFAN BOGNER
BEN WINTER

ART DIRECTION, LAYOUT,
FOTOS/ART DIRECTION,
LAYOUT, PHOTOS:
STEFAN BOGNER

BILDER THEREME VALS:
© 7132 HOTEL & GLOBAL
IMAGE CREATION

TEXT/TEXT: BEN WINTER
TEXT INTRO/TEXT INTRO:
BEN WINTER

MOTIVAUSARBEITUNG
LITHOGRAPHIE/SATZ/

POST-PRODUCTION,
LITHOGRAPHY/SETTING:
MICHAEL DORN

KARTENMATERIAL/MAP
MATERIAL: MAIRDUMONT,
OSTFILDERN

ÜBERSETZUNG/TRANSLATION
JAMES O'NEILL

PRODUKTIONSLEITUNG/
PRODUCTION MANAGEMENT:
AXEL GERBER

DRUCK/PRINT:
PRINT BEST
VILJANDI, ESTLAND

2. AUFLAGE/2ND EDITION:
ISBN: 978-3-667-12158-5

AUSGEZEICHNET MIT / AWARDED WITH
DDC GOLD - DEUTSCHER DESIGNER CLUB E.V. FÜR GUTE GESTALTUNG // IF COMMUNICATION DESIGN AWARD 2012 BEST OF CORPORATE PUBLISHING // ADC BRONZE // RED DOT BEST OF THE BEST & D&AD // NOMINIERT FÜR DEN DEUTSCHEN DESIGNPREIS 2015 // WINNER AUTOMOTIVE BRAND CONTEST 2014 // GOOD DESIGN AWARD 2014

CURVES AUSGABEN / OTHER ISSUES OF CURVES

PYRENÄEN / PYRENEES
Im Handel erhältlich/Available in stores

ÖSTERREICH / AUSTRIA
Im Handel erhältlich/Available in stores

SCHWEIZ / SWITZERLAND
Im Handel erhältlich/Available in stores

SCHOTTLAND / SCOTLAND
Im Handel erhältlich/Available in stores

FRANKREICH / FRANCE
Im Handel erhältlich/Available in stores

USA · KALIFORNIEN / USA · CALIFORNIA
Im Handel erhältlich/Available in stores

SIZILIEN / SICILY
Im Handel erhältlich/Available in stores

NORDITALIEN / NORTHERN ITALY
Im Handel erhältlich/Available in stores

OSTDEUTSCHLAND / EASTERN GERMANY
Im Handel erhältlich/Available in stores

DEUTSCHLAND/DÄNEMARK / GERMANY/DENMARK
Im Handel erhältlich/Available in stores

NEUSEELAND / NEW ZEALAND
Im Handel erhältlich/Available in stores

SARDINIEN / SARDINIA
Im Handel erhältlich/Available in stores

SPANIEN · MALLORCA / SPAIN · MALLORCA
Im Handel erhältlich/Available in stores

USA · COLORADO/UTAH / USA · COLORADO/UTAH
Im Handel erhältlich/Available in stores

THAILAND / THAILAND
Im Handel erhältlich/Available in stores

SÜDDEUTSCHLAND / SOUTHERN GERMANY
Im Handel erhältlich/Available in stores

PORTUGAL / PORTUGAL
Im Handel erhältlich/Available in stores

ISLAND / ICELAND
Im Handel erhältlich/Available in stores

MALAYSIA / MALAYSIA
Im Handel erhältlich/Available in stores

NORWEGEN / NORWAY
Im Handel erhältlich/Available in stores

PATAGONIEN / PATAGONIA
Im Handel erhältlich/Available in stores

KORSIKA / CORSICA
Im Handel erhältlich/Available in stores

SINGAPUR / SINGAPORE
Im Handel erhältlich/Available in stores

JAPAN / JAPAN
Im Handel erhältlich/Available in stores

Eine Liebeserklärung an die Kurve.
Der 911 GT3 mit Touring-Paket.
Mehr unter www.porsche.de/GT3TouringPaket
PORSCHE
S TP 992
Kraftstoffverbrauch in l/100 km: innerorts 19,1–17,3 · außerorts 10,0–9,5 · kombiniert 13,3–12,4 (NEFZ); kombiniert 12,9 (WLTP);
CO_2-Emissionen in g/km kombiniert: 304–283 (NEFZ); 293–292 (WLTP); Stand 10/2021